writer TO writer

Books by Cecil Murphey Include...

- *Unleash the Writer Within*

- *Writer to Writer: Lessons from a Lifetime of Writing*

- *The Promises of Ophelia Bennett* (fiction)

- *90 Minutes in Heaven* (with Don Piper)

- *A Walk through the Dark: How My Husband's 90 Minutes in Heaven Deepened My Faith for a Lifetime* (with Eva Piper)

- *Gifted Hands: The Ben Carson Story* (with Dr. Ben Carson)

- *Not Quite Healed: 40 Truths for Male Survivors of Childhood Sexual Abuse* (by Cecil Murphey and Gary Roe)

- *Saying Goodbye: Facing the Death of a Loved One* (by Cecil Murphey and Gary Roe)

- *I Believe in Healing: Real Stories from the Bible, History and Today* (by Cecil Murphey and Twila Belk)

- *I Believe in Heaven: Real Stories from the Bible, History and Today* (by Cecil Murphey and Twila Belk)

- *Making Sense When Life Doesn't: The Secrets of Thriving in Tough Times*

- *Heavenly Company: Entertaining Angels Unaware* (by Cecil Murphey and Twila Belk)

- *Knowing God, Knowing Myself: An Invitation to Daily Discovery*

- *When a Man You Love Was Abused: A Woman's Guide to Helping Him Overcome Childhood Sexual Molestation*

- *When Someone You Love No Longer Remembers*

- *Because You Care: Spiritual Encouragement for Caregivers* (by Cecil Murphey and Twila Belk)

writer TO writer

Lessons from a Lifetime of Writing

CECIL MURPHEY

OAKTARA
www.oaktara.com

Writer to Writer

Published in the U.S. by:
OakTara Publishers
P.O. Box 8, Waterford, VA 20197
www.oaktara.com

Cover design by Yvonne Parks at www.pearcreative.ca
Cover image © thinkstockphotos.ca: book sellout/iStockphoto collection,
93171259.

Published in association with: Deidre Knight of The Knight Agency, Inc., 570
East Avenue, Madison, GA 30650; http://www.knightagency.net/.

Unless otherwise indicated, all Scripture quotations are taken from the Holy
Bible, New Living Translation, copyright 1996, 2004, 2007 by Tyndale House
Foundation. Used by permission of Tyndale House Publishers, Inc., Carol
Stream, Illinois 06188, USA. All rights reserved.

ISBN-13: 978-1-60290-376-0
ISBN-10: 1-60290-376-X

Printed in the U.S.A.

Contents

* * *

INTRODUCTION

Why This Book?

THIS ISN'T A GRAMMAR BOOK.

This isn't a rulebook for writers.

This is an attempt to share the lessons I've learned as a professional writer. Nothing else.

I can't recall when I didn't want to write. Although I tried to get published at age sixteen, I had nothing accepted until I was thirty-eight. By then, I had learned a few things about the publishing industry.

After I had sold at least twenty articles, I made a double commitment.

First, I promised God and myself that I would never stop learning and improving as a writer.

Second, I promised I would do whatever I could to help other writers.

Most of the material in *Writer to Writer* started as a blog in 2011. It represents my commitment to continue to improve and shows the results of my learning that have enabled me to partially fulfill the second part of the commitment.

For years, I've cringed when I read shoddy writing in print, especially in those instances that would take little effort to improve the quality.

I want to help *you* become better; however, you'll discover no easy path to writing success. Good writing demands self-discipline and constant learning.

I've tried to keep each entry in *Writer to Writer* short and well illustrated. From my teaching experience in my own mentoring clinics, I figured out that receiving large globs of information over a period of two or three days has little effect.

That's why I started the blog. By throwing about 200 to 300 words at writers twice a week, my assumption is that they would be able to absorb what they learned before moving on to the next blog entry.

I've revised the blogs into a book with the same objective. Read an entry a day or five in a week. You can jump into the book any place you like and get the message in about two minutes each time.

I also confess that writing this book is a defensive action. My assistant, Twila Belk, and one of my writing cronies, Jim Rubart, urged me to share what I've learned about writing. Hence, the tagline supplied by Jim: *Lessons from a lifetime of writing.*

I'm still learning.

My goal is to send in manuscripts that make editors weep and tell me, "I couldn't find a single thing to change." In the meantime, I pass on what I've learned from my years of professional writing. I trust it will help you, too.

1

* * *

Beyond
the Amateur Look

Don't Remain an Amateur

*

UNLESS YOU HAVE ESTABLISHED A RELATIONSHIP WITH AN EDITOR, you won't send a manuscript without permission.

"We look for reasons to reject manuscripts," an editor-friend said.

I understood what she meant. Editors are overwhelmed, and their staffs are smaller these days. More people now try to write, and many of them send multiple submissions for the same article. Instead of getting 300 manuscripts a month as book publishers might have twenty years ago, those same publishers receive 300 a week.

Good editors easily eliminate a high percentage of the submissions without reading a word. They need only to look at the layout. "Amateurs won't take time to learn to submit a book proposal properly," another editor complained.

Most publishers provide guidelines on their website. Despite that, a large number of articles and books come to publishers that show the writers haven't followed their guidelines.

Think of it this way: If you send in a manuscript that deviates from the standard look, it's enough to cause an editor to blink. The blink encourages the editor to put the pages in the reject basket.

I want to offer guidelines to help you get your manuscript read. This will avoid the initial rejection, and the editors might actually buy what you've submitted. The guidelines are easy to follow and simple to learn.

I'll do everything I can to prejudice editors in my favor by making my manuscript look professional.

The Basics on Manuscripts

*

1. DOUBLE-SPACE ALL MANUSCRIPTS and leave a one-inch margin on all sides of the page. (This is automatic on most computers.) Don't insert extra blank lines between paragraphs.

2. Use a header on every page. On the left, the header contains your last name, slant or colon, and your title. Put the page number on the right. (I put my header in 9-point font so that it becomes less distracting.)

It's not wrong, but I suggest you avoid putting the header on the first page. It's simple to do. On your tool bar, go to *Insert.* On the pull-down menu you'll see *Page Numbers.* Delete the checkmark that says to start on page 1.

3. Indent every paragraph half an inch. (Set your tab key. In Word, you need to hit the space bar ten times to get half an inch.) Always use 12-point fonts. Many prefer non-serif fonts such as my favorite, Arial. Don't use italics, or difficult-to-read fonts. Times New Roman (TNR) is the most common and is the default font on Word. If the publisher's guidelines don't tell you which font, TNR is a safe font.

Because I'm a serious writer,
I pay attention to the basics.

Don't Shout Your Amateur Status

*

NONPROFESSIONALS INSERT THE COPYRIGHT SYMBOL on the first page and some do it on every page. Editors know (even if writers don't) that the material is under common-law copyright when the piece is in a finished form.

Using the symbol is a not-so-subtle way to say to editors, "I'm afraid you'll steal my words, so this is my warning." As one editor told me, "Those who use the copyright symbol rarely have to worry about anyone wanting to steal from them. Their writing is usually terrible."

I make my manuscript look professional so editors will treat me like a professional.

Follow the Established Format

*

THE NORMAL FORMAT FOR MANUSCRIPTS has been standard for many years.

1. In the upper left corner of the first page, *single space on separate lines,* your name, address, phone number, and email address. (I'm amazed at the people who don't show editors how to contact them.)

2. Across from your name, in the upper right, give an *estimated* word count, rounded off to the nearest 50. To write 937 words is not an estimate, but 950 is. Even a small thing like that shouts "Beginner."

3. On the next line, put the rights you want to sell. For articles, this will usually be first rights. (*First rights* mean that after they have published it once, it's yours to resell.) The top of your first page, the only single spacing you do in an article, will look like this:

My name	About 1,000 words
Address	First Rights Only
Address	
Phone and Email	

4. Once you've put in your information at the top of the page, go down about 1/3 of the page and center the title. (I usually begin at 3.8 inches or four inches, but the exact number isn't important.) That empty space between your personal information and the title of the article is reserved for the editor. Don't put anything in that space.

5. After you've centered your title, hit "Enter" and start typing. (You don't need to put "by…" because it's at the top of the page and your name is in your header on every subsequent page.

6. When you get to the end, just stop. You don't need anything like -30- or "The End."

When editors see no more words, they're intelligent enough to know that you've finished. (And your manuscript will feel complete.)

It takes little effort for my manuscripts to look professional, but it does take effort.

The Natural Sound

*

DURING THE PAST FEW YEARS many writers have begun putting the verb (said, replied, answered) before the speaker. "What do you want?" asked Mary.

It's not wrong, but it's not a natural way of speaking. I enjoy children's stories because of the rhythm.

For example, the Little Red Hen asks who will help her bake the bread.

"Not I," barked the lazy dog.

"Not I," quacked the noisy yellow duck.

This works in the read-aloud story "The Little Red Hen" because it propels the story and listeners get caught up in the rhythm. But as the great theologian Paul wrote, "But when I grew up, I put away childish things" (1 Corinthians 13:11b).

"What do you want?" Mary asked.

"I don't know," Kelly answered.

Good writing is natural and keeps readers focused on the dialog and not on the writing style.

The more natural my writing,
the easier it is to read.

Simple English?

*

HERE'S A STATEMENT I ABSORBED IN MY EARLY DAYS OF WRITING, and I still believe it: The most powerful words tend to be the shortest and most basic to the English language. Don't try to impress with your vocabulary. You write to communicate—to connect with your readers.

You may use a word that every reader won't know, but if you do it well, they'll grasp the meaning from the context (but use sparingly).

George Orwell's essay "Politics and the English Language"[1] contrasts a well-known verse from Ecclesiastes with his own satirical translation:

> Objective considerations of contemporary phenomena compel the conclusion that success or failure in competitive activities exhibits no tendency to be commensurate with innate capacity, but that a considerable element of the unpredictable must invariably be taken into account.

Here is the same verse, Ecclesiastes 9:11, in a modern translation: "I have seen something else under the sun: The race is not to the swift or the battle to the strong, nor does food come to the wise or wealth to the brilliant or favor to the learned; but time and chance happen to them all."[2]

Write to develop a relationship with your readers. You want to enlighten, entertain, or encourage them. That is, you want to communicate. You can't do that if you try to impress them and ignore common words they understand.

> Because I write to communicate,
> I avoid writing to impress my readers.

---

[1] As cited by Helen Sword, http://opinionator.blogs.nytimes.com/2012/07/23/zombie-nouns/?ref=opinion.

[2] The Holy Bible, *Today's New International Version,* TNIV, 2005.

Inclusive Language

*

MAN NO LONGER MEANS *HUMANITY.* Be sensitive to the role of women. It's still being used and some people resent and resist the change. But some of them still use typewriters and VHS.

- The first generation of man…It takes little to shift to the first human generation or the first generation of humanity.
- Manning *[staffing]* the helm as we crossed a stretch of the Atlantic Ocean.
- A family of Orientals *[Asians]* lives across the street from us.

We no longer use ethnic slurs, so let's be consistent. (We used to write *racial slurs.*)

Because I am a caring, sensitive writer,
I avoid offending readers.

Amateur Words

*

LET'S LOOK AT TWO WORDS AMATEURS LOVE TO INSERT (and I did in my early days). So here's the rule: Don't use speed words unless it's important to stress the time factor.

- His eyes adjusted *quickly* to the murky light.
- Elmer made a *quick* survey of the narrow room. (Same principle: If he surveys a room, unless there is reason for haste, wouldn't he do it slowly and methodically? Isn't that the idea of surveying?)
- She shuddered and *hurriedly* smiled an apology.

I omit speed words from my writing unless I want to emphasize haste.

First Words, First Paragraphs
PART 1 OF 7

*

OUR INITIAL WORDS NEED TO MAKE AN IMMEDIATE APPEAL TO READERS. Perhaps that's obvious, but some authors assume that if readers stay with them, the rest of the book will reward them.

If readers stay with them. That assumes they will. Don't deceive yourself. Your first duty is to grab their attention and make them yearn for more. That's your responsibility.

Pique my interest.

Promise me that you can help me with my immediate problem.

Make me care about a character.

Tickle me so that I'll chuckle.

Many writers agonize over that initial sentence; some should agonize more. If you don't get the first words right, the rest of the writing won't matter: No one will read it.

Over the years I've asked editors and agents how much of a manuscript they read before they make a decision. Most of them tell me that if the first paragraph is badly written, that's enough and they reject it. Some agents allow them only a full page. They're busy and they won't belabor manuscripts they'll reject anyway.

One agent hires a first reader to go through all submissions. "If you're still reading after page 4," she told her reader, "I want to see it." That means that the prospective client has to have a strong beginning or the agent herself never sees the manuscript.

Unfair? I've heard that complaint. Perhaps to you, but this is business— big business. Why would an agent want to read fifty pages of a book she will reject anyway?

When I used to do mentoring clinics, I asked everyone to send me only the first five pages. Even though I could have asked for less, I wanted to get a feel for the manuscript. The weaknesses of the first paragraphs aren't unique to that page. They're normally the same weaknesses that flow through the rest of the manuscript.

Think of it this way. In your first sentence (and certainly within the first paragraph) you make a contract with your readers. You imply, "If you read this, you'll be entertained, informed, motivated, or receive emotional satisfaction."

That's your promise and you need to fulfill that commitment. Work on those first words. Tradition says Plato rewrote the first sentence fifty times for *The Republic.*

I work to make the first sentence easy to read. That's also my promise about the rest of the manuscript.

First Words, First Paragraphs

*

I'VE COME UP WITH SEVERAL WAYS TO START A MANUSCRIPT.

The first and most basic rule is *show and don't tell.* Let your reader see or feel something. My late friend, Charlie Shedd, wrote a book about forty years ago called *Pray Your Weight Away.* (Good, catchy title.) Here is his first sentence: "Three years and one hundred pounds ago I dropped to my knees and prayed."

This simple sentence *shows* us something without explaining. Charlie's simple sentence does several things:

- It grabs attention.
- It starts in an imaginative way. (He could have written, "I was an up-and-down dieter until I prayed.")
- He hints at the problem (weight).
- He promises a solution (prayer).

Good beginnings invite readers to continue
and hint at what will follow.

First Words, First Paragraphs

*

HERE'S THE SECOND RULE: *Good beginnings thrust readers into the problem.* Your responsibility is to make readers sense the tension or the action. I think of the first line as saying to readers, "Here's a situation that we're going to solve."

The implied promise can be solving a crime, loving again after rejection, raising healthy, happy children, or spying during World War II. Whether fiction or nonfiction, the principle is the same.

Jane Austen's novel, *Pride and Prejudice* begins, "It is a truth universally acknowledged, that a single man in possession of a good fortune, must be in want of a wife." Those words carry a light, humorous tone and readers get it immediately. And we get it in reverse: women seek husbands with money. (The publication date was 1813, in a male-controlled society, so you can accept her attitude about marriage.)

Here's the first line from the nonfiction book, *90 Minutes in Heaven,* that I wrote for Don Piper: "I died on January 18, 1989."

Died? If Don Piper died, how could he be alive now to tell of his death? That's what we call the hook—something to pull readers into your writing.

Here's the first sentence from my book *When a Man You Love Was Abused:* "He was molested—or at least you suspect he was." That hints at the problem.

In the three examples above, each makes you aware of an issue, and you want to make readers *participants* in your book. You want them to travel with you until you arrive at a satisfactory outcome.

By contrast, weak beginnings often start with information about the weather ("In June, the heat began to hit New Yorkers."), or the time of day ("I awakened and it was still dark.") Neither example compels us to read further.

> Good beginnings provide a problem
> and promise to solve it.

First Words, First Paragraphs

PART 4 OF 7

*

GOOD BEGINNINGS TELL YOU THE TYPE OF BOOK OR ARTICLE. From the first paragraph readers need to know whether it's biography, slice-of-life, mystery, romance, or tragedy.

The first sentence sets the tone for what will follow.

"My problems date back to the day I ate my brother's live goldfish." Just that much of a made-up beginning tells me I'll probably read humor.

The first chapter of Spero Pastos, *Pin-Up: The Tragedy of Betty Grable* begins: "Betty Grable's mother was determined to make her daughter a star."[3]

These two sentences begin my novel *Everybody Called Her a Saint:* "If it hadn't been for Twila Belk, I wouldn't have taken the Antarctic cruise, and I wouldn't have seen Burton again. If I hadn't gone on the cruise, I wouldn't have been there when someone murdered Twila."

Compare the difference, especially in the tone of these three examples. Doesn't the type of book seem obvious? One is humor, another is an impersonal, biography of a movie star, and the third is a murder mystery. Most readers pick that up immediately, even though they may not consciously realize it.

> Smart writers make readers aware
> of the type of writing and its tone.

---

[3] *Pin-Up: The Tragedy of Betty Grable,* Spero Pastos (New York: Berkley, 1987) p. 3.

First Words, First Paragraphs

*

THIS MAY SOUND STRANGE, but *readers need an element of time as quickly as possible*. This is crucial *with fiction*. We assume it is the present time unless you make it clear that it's not.

Some authors set it up by writing something like: Nairobi, Kenya, April 1935, at the top of the first page of chapter one. That's not extremely imaginative, but it makes readers aware.

David Morrell's novel *Long Lost* doesn't give us a date, but we realize the time period: "When I was a boy, my kid brother disappeared. Vanished off the face of the earth."[4] Because of the way Morrell starts the book, we assume we're talking anywhere from ten to thirty years before the present. That's good enough to ease us into the time period.

Here's the general rule about historical fiction or nonfiction: Make the time period clear within the first sentence or at least by the end of the opening paragraph. In *His Excellency George Washington,* Joseph J. Ellis makes the period clear with these words: "History first noticed George Washington in 1753, as a daring and resourceful twenty-one-year-old messenger sent on a dangerous mission into the American wilderness."[5]

My beginnings clarify the time period before readers have to ask, "When does this take place?"

---

[4] *Long Lost,* David Morrell (Warner, 2002), p. 3.
[5] *His Excellency George Washington,* Joseph J. Ellis (New York: Knopf, 2004), p. 3.

First Words, First Paragraphs

*

IF THE TIME ELEMENT IS IMPORTANT (and it is), the *sense of place is of equal significance.* You don't have to say the story starts in San Francisco or Atlanta, but give us a hint. Show us a busy street or an apartment. Do we hear carriage wheels? Is that a bugle playing "Taps"? Make it clear if the story starts at a hotel, airport, police station, or a mansion.

For me, it's like waking up out of a deep sleep and asking myself, *Where am I?* I wouldn't ask that question if I were in my own bed, but if I awakened in a hammock or on a mud floor, I might.

I make readers aware of the place to ease them into reading the rest.

First Words, First Paragraphs

*

"HOW LONG SHOULD A BEGINNING BE?" I hear that question often. By beginning, they usually refer to setting up the book so readers will plunge into it.

Here are my answers. First, no one can prescribe length. Each time it's different. Much of it depends on the type of material, your purpose in writing, and how technical your material.

Second, keep it as short as possible. Immediately I think of "Life is difficult," the first words of *The Road Less Traveled.* Those three words set up the problem of the book and M. Scott Peck implies, "I know your life is tough and I want to show you how to cope."

Third, make your opening not only quick to read, but easy to read. If I pick up a book and I have to stumble through the first paragraph, I'll probably close the book.

Here's the most important rule I know in beginnings: *Readers are interested in themselves.* They want to be entertained or enlightened. They want you to solve a problem or show them how to make life more livable.

I decide the length of my beginnings;
at the same time, I consider my readers' interests.

Don't Bore Your Readers

YOU CAN'T BORE READERS: THEY'LL STOP READING. Perhaps that sounds obvious, but too many writers are fascinated with their topic—usually their own lives—and assume everyone else cares. If you write as a form of therapy (and that's valid), and recognize what you're doing, you don't try to push the rest of the world to read and care about your struggles.

Some writers assume readers are eager to grasp every word they write. The opposite is true: You have to persuade people to read your work and assure them that the time they spend with you will be rewarding.

You do that at the start of your manuscript. What promises do you make in your title? in your first sentence? your opening paragraph?

When you forget readers, you invite them to close the book. Whether you're entertaining or teaching, people read because of their perceived needs. You write to meet those needs.

Because *you* find it interesting or think your life is newsworthy, it's easy to assume everyone cares. It's better to *assume no one cares about what you write.* Your first task is to give readers reasons to care—early in the article or book—and keep them interested because you relate to their lives.

> If I put the needs of readers first,
> I earn the right to be read.

Write, Write,
and Write Some More

*

WOULD-BE-WRITERS OFTEN ASK WHETHER THEY SHOULD WRITE EVERY DAY. Instead of answering, here's my question: Why wouldn't you *yearn* to write every day? You may not do it *every day* of the year, but you do it as often and as faithfully as possible. You form the writing habit, which is called self-discipline.

I began my career with the commitment to write at least 15 minutes every day. That was all the time I could comfortably squeeze from my life. (Within six months, I was writing an hour a day.)

If your goal is to be a great hitter, you swing the baseball bat every day; opera singers sing every day; writers write every day—every day and at every opportunity. Nothing improves your writing more than working at it faithfully.

If you write on a regular basis, you'll probably improve. Not everyone does, because some refuse to learn. They keep turning out the same mediocrity year after year.

You can write at noon or nighttime, in the bedroom and the snack room, on Saturdays and stolen moments.

But write. Write faithfully.

Like me, you may write fast, or you may be a slow, plodding writer. It doesn't matter. Just write.

Do you want to be a good writer? Then write. If you want to write well and sell much, write much.

> Because I want to be a good writer,
> here are three things I do regularly:
> I write, write, and write.

Rewrite

*

THE BEST WRITING IS REWRITING—which isn't an original comment. That means not being easily satisfied and constantly sensing you can make your prose better. Working hard and learning to rewrite makes you sharper and more coherent. That's what moves writers into the professional level.

When you rewrite, you rethink what you've written. You admit that some words feel exactly right and you leave them. You delete sentences that don't flow or add words for clarity.

I say it this way: I write subjectively; I edit objectively. That means that on my first draft I let words flow without censoring or interrupting. Once I finish I go back and objectively correct what I've written.

Effective rewriting is a skill I learn
by going through the process hundreds of times.

Read. A Lot. Often. Constantly.

*

IF YOU'RE A SERIOUS WRITER, YOU READ and you do so in a variety of areas, always seeking to know more about writing and about your world. You read in your genre, but you also read outside your field.

Too often, I meet want-to-be writers who don't read—some don't like to read—and yet they feel they must write. That doesn't make sense to me. Someone said it's like hating horses while raising herds of them and lecturing around the country on how to love your animal. It's not only hypocritical; it won't work.

Professional writers don't *like* to read—they're compulsive and *must* read. They snatch minutes whenever possible to fill their eyes and minds with words and new thoughts.

Words are your tools and you constantly examine their meanings. You feel them and learn to distinguish between *small, little, tiny, miniscule,* or *minute.* You read and pick up nuances of meaning, marvel at the expressive efforts of others, or groan at the lack of skill in your own manuscripts.

You absorb techniques and ideas when you read, mostly unconsciously. You become absorbed and challenged by writers who are better than you are. *And there are always writers who are superior.*

You read for pleasure, but even then, you read to learn. Every article or book you read becomes a teacher. As you read, you ask questions, often unconsciously. Why did she start the story there? What does *that word* mean? Why did he use the subjunctive mood?

I am a compulsive reader, and that makes me a better writer.

Grow Professionally

*

LEARN THE CRAFT—AND KEEP LEARNING. Strive to become the best writer possible and there's no rest stop on your highway.

Growing professionally means an unrelenting search for excellence. You're never satisfied. You smile when you construct a good paragraph and say to yourself, I'll continue to improve.

Here's something else you can do for yourself: Connect with other writers, those who will nudge you to push yourself. You don't want to connect just to get someone to taunt you until you finish an article or book. Why not covenant with another to push you to make your manuscript the best writing you can do at this stage of your development?

If you're serious, *development* is the ongoing objective.

> I'm never fully satisfied with my writing
> because I know I can improve.

Mimic the Best

*

I CAN'T SAY THIS ENOUGH: IMITATE THE WRITERS YOU ADMIRE. Would-be basketball heroes copy the moves of the players they admire.

For example, when I was fifteen years old I first read William Saroyan's *The Human Comedy*. I didn't know anything about professional writing, but I knew two things. First, I wanted to write. Second, I wanted to write with Saroyan's warmth.

I've done the first and I'm still working on the second. Saroyan's writing gave me permission to express my heart on paper. That's one kind of imitation.

The other is to copy their words. When you read something that makes you pause and say, "I wish I had written that," write or type the words. File them. Read them occasionally. As you copy and ponder the prose, you're absorbing their style.

Don't merely copy best-selling writers. I can think of several top-grossing writers, but it's not their mastery of the craft that makes them sell; it's probably their plots or the material they cover.

I started with two writers I liked, and neither of whom were in my field. That didn't matter and may have been a positive factor. I couldn't steal or copy their prose, but I learned better phrasing and different ways to express thoughts.

I read more advanced writers;
I imitate them so that I can become better than they are.

Insulting Readers

*

DON'T INSULT YOUR READERS. By that I mean, don't state the obvious.

I see this occur in two different ways. First, some writers are so eager to be understood they'll give the same information in different words, as in this example: "I ran with haste; I ignored everyone on the street as I hurried. I refused to stop when anyone waved."

Stop! I understood the first time. This person is running fast. Do I need to read it three times to figure it out?

Second, they write a good, show-not-tell sentence and follow it up with the same information in a tell-but-not-show sentence.

- The urgency and agony in his voice was unmistakable, and it was the saddest sound I'd heard from him. Something was terribly wrong. (The second sentence implies I'm too stupid to know the meaning of words like *urgency, agony,* and *sad.*)
- I couldn't speak; I could not tell her what was happening. (If I couldn't speak, I assume that means I couldn't use words to explain.)
- It was a stunning, tremendous, blazing bright meteor! It dwarfed all other stars in the sky, making the pinpricks of their light barely visible. It immediately commanded our attention, holding Renee and me spellbound. (The author gave the meteor more attention than I would have in this badly written paragraph.)
- Shouldn't we prepare ourselves in advance to face them? (Or do we prepare ourselves afterward?)
- The impact totaled the car and left Amy's body broken, bruised, and with a collapsed lung. She was in grave physical danger. (The second sentence insults me by saying I don't understand the seriousness of the injuries.)

Readers are as smart as I am;
therefore I refuse to write obvious statements.

Meaningless Words

*

DELETE WORDS THAT ADD NO VALUE TO A SENTENCE, such as *some, really, very, just, managed to*, and *at all*. They're not wrong, but they add nothing.

What's the difference between he was dead and he was very dead? She drank some coffee or she drank coffee?

- Today's news, though, called for *some* serious grime-fighting—scouring baseboards. (You can usually delete *some* without hurting your sentence.)
- She'd *managed to* arrive at the law office before anyone. (She arrived…)
- The tension in his jaw *began to* cause a noticeable ache, but he ignored it. (The tension caused his jaw to ache.)
- Jessica was *really* nervous about mentioning Jervus to Amanda, and she didn't *really even* know why. (Really, really.)
- My world had *very* abruptly come to an end.
- Both of my sons were *just* waiting for the phone call.
- He wasn't dead *at all.*
- They stopped for *some* fast food.

I write concisely,
so I delete words that add no value to a sentence.

Fewer Words

*

WHAT'S WRONG WITH SAYING *baby puppies* and *dead meat?* I assume you know the answer—they're redundant. Puppies are babies and all meat is dead. One word is enough.

I watch for and get rid of unneeded words.

I went to his house in order to get his autograph. Delete *in order* and the sentence makes sense with fewer words: I went to his house to get his autograph.

- She didn't know whether or not she would attend the meeting. Delete *or not,* which is implied by the word *whether.* She didn't know whether she would attend the meeting.

Here are additional examples:

- Appear on the scene...[change to]...appear
- Bring to a conclusion...conclude
- Bring with you...bring
- enclosed here with...enclosed
- Explicitly state...state
- Make a motion...move
- Substitute in her place...substitute
- Any and all...any [or] all (use one)
- Each and every...each [or] every (use one)
- In this day and age...today [or] now (use one)
- Many in number...many
- Green in color...green
- Due to the fact...because

To make my writing clear,
I use the fewest number of words.

Absolutes

*

AVOID THE ABSOLUTES—unless you mean *without exception*. You can usually delete the absolute and not change the intended meaning.

- You know how I've *always* felt about going into debt. (Always? Since the moment of birth? Better: You know how I feel about going into debt.)
- *All* Twinkles ever wanted was... (That's all? Just one thing?)
- He made his *every* movement appear as...
- This morning, *all* he wanted to do...
- Weekends were always busy. (If there was one un-busy weekend, *always* isn't always.)
- I walked around with *total* freedom.
- Joy is what this life is all about. (Is there nothing else in life?)
- Every one of my married friends told me. (Are you sure that without exception *every* married friend told you?)
- Every human makes mistakes. (Here the absolute is correct.)

I avoid absolutes
when I write.

Don't Confuse Best-selling Authors with Best-written Books

*

MOST OF US KNOW WRITERS WHO SELL BIG but it's in spite of their weak writing.

Here are two examples:

1. In David Balducci's *Simple Genius,* a therapist talks to Michelle. The paragraph reads: "Michelle looked nervously away." He's a famous author, so what does that say?[6]

Answer: It says he got away with it. Being a best-selling author doesn't equal being an excellent writer. The sentence itself is awkward. He could have written: Michelle looked away nervously. (Nervously and away are adverbs and adverbs can modify other adverbs. As written nervously modifies *away,* which I assume isn't the author's intent.) Also, this isn't written in Michelle's point of view, so how does the protagonist know it's a nervous gesture?

Aside from grammar, he *told* us, and how do we, the readers, know what *nervous* is? We can read into the book words that aren't there, but (tsk tsk), Baldacci could have done better.

2. A famous author wrote a single sentence of dialog and added, "He asked curiously." That's clumsy writing because *curiously* doesn't show us anything. Does the writer mean the man spoke in an odd way? Does he mean the man was inquisitive?

> Bad writing appears in print.
> I don't want to add to it;
> I want to be a corrective voice.

---

[6] *Simple Genius,* David Balducci (Vision, 2008), p. 97.

Italics for Titles

*

"GONE WITH THE WIND" served as the theme for those five weekends.

In the movie "The Dark Knight"...

Growing up, my favorite TV series was: Eight Is Enough.

All three are incorrect. It's *Gone with the Wind.* In pre-computer days, you would have underlined because typewriters couldn't make italics. Editors understood the underlinings.

When you refer to chapters, poems, segments of a TV series, use quotation marks.

My favorite poem is "Alone" by Edgar Allan Poe.

Weekends with Larry aired a piece called "Five Good Movies to Watch."

Because I'm a serious writer,
I know when to use italics and
when to use quotation marks in titles.

Those Clichés

*

CLICHÉS ARE THOSE TIRED, OVERWORKED PHRASES that you hear and read constantly. It's easy to write with hackneyed expressions because you don't have to work hard and you sound like everyone else.

A major difference between mediocre authors and excellent ones is that the former use the current expressions of the day and they sound like everyone else instead of trying to say it in their own words.

The cliché can be a simple word (*utilize* instead of *use)*, or a phrase (*at the end of the day, at this point in time,* or *do the math*).

Here are a few. I have collected several hundred of them. (Or I could use the hackneyed clause *I have literally hundreds of them.*)

- The searing pain returned in full blast;
- With each passing second;
- The last thing I wanted was;
- It was marvelous to behold;
- To take the edge off;
- I was frozen for what seemed like an eternity;
- More than I cared to know;
- I'll defend it tooth and nail;
- Spoiling for a fight;
- The defining moment of my life.

I used to belong to three *professional* writers loops. For just *one day* I jotted down the clichés that flowed through their postings. I quit after about twenty posts. Those writers were probably unaware of the tired expressions, but they used phrases that required little effort.

One woman told me, "I'm more careful when I write for print." I didn't argue with her, but when you post isn't that writing for print? If you attempt to be careful in everything you write, you don't have to worry about shifting from not caring to careful.

Here are a few of those I found on the three professional writers loops.

- Feel free to;
- For whatever reason;
- Bored to tears;

- I'll chime in later;
- My two cents' worth;
- The key to.

I remind myself that clichés work for easy writing;
cliché also make for boring reading.

Correct Emphasis

*

IN PRE-COMPUTER DAYS, WRITERS EMPHASIZED WORDS by using quotation marks. These days, if you want to emphasize a word, use italics or boldface. Put words in quotes only if readers might otherwise misunderstand.

- Do you have a "giant" in your life that needs tackling right now?
- She will suffer through the "cold turkey" routine.
- He'll show them through this "chance" event.
- Eldred aims to come up with persuasive "arguments" when confronting difficult reasons.
- I had never felt that mysterious "knowledge."

If you use words in a special or different sense, for clarity you use quotation marks.

Here is an example where you would use quotation marks for clarity: In filmmaking, movable "wild walls" make a room seem to have four walls.

If readers understand the meaning,
I delete quotation marks meant for emphasis.

Shorten Those Sentences

*

GRUMBLE IF YOU LIKE, but terse-and-clear is the mark of good writing.

Whether or not you think a sentence is too short, in order to write well, it probably isn't too short at all.

Read that 22-word sentence again. You can cut words. Whether implies *or not*. *At all* is redundant and you can cut *in order*. I'd suggest you make the sentence read this way: *If you think a sentence is too short, it probably isn't.* Not only is the revision shorter, but it's clearer and more readily understood.

When I first started to write, the late Charlie Shedd taught, "Never make a sentence longer than 15 words." His rule seemed arbitrary. In those days 50 words wasn't too long for a sentence. Yet I vigilantly limited my sentences so I didn't exceed that number. After a time, however, I realized that 15 makes choppy writing.

Here's how I say it today: "Let your sentences *average* no more than 20 words." Good writing doesn't demand a word limit on a sentence. Take as long as you need to express a thought. Afterward, go back and eliminate words or perhaps revise a long sentence into two.

If you write succinctly and clearly, you're one rung higher on the good-writer ladder. You can figure out the antithesis of that statement. *Antithesis* is a good word, but it may be beyond the vocabulary of some readers. Why not say *the opposite?* That's another tip.

Good writers cut ruthlessly.
Because I am becoming a good writer, I cut ruthlessly.

It Is and There Was

*

YOU PROBABLY WON'T FIND THIS PRINCIPLE IN A TEXTBOOK, but I urge you to avoid starting sentences with these: *there is, it is, there is,* and *there was.* Avoid them for one reason: They're weak words. You can usually delete them for a better sentence flow.

- It was Saturday at the animal shelter, and it was alive with the... (Saturday at the shelter...or, People scurried/bustled/hurried Saturday morning at the...)
- It was a spring weekend and we drove to Maine. (On a spring weekend... or, We drove to Maine on a spring weekend.)
- It was a time when I had no other place to turn. (Better: I had no place to turn.)
- There's a van coming right at us. (A van is coming right at us.)

When I teach about not starting with those words, a few students remind me that Dickens began *A Tale of Two Cities* with that construction. He did it for effect—and the lyrical tone. His novel starts with these words:

"It was the best of times, it was the worst of times, it was the age of wisdom, it was the age of foolishness, it was the epoch of belief, it was the epoch of incredulity, it was the season of Light, it was the season of Darkness, it was the spring of hope, it was the winter of despair..."

If I avoid starting sentences with constructions
such as *it was* or *there was,*
my writing is stronger.

Identify *It*

*

WRITERS GET SO CAUGHT UP IN THEIR WRITING they don't always make the antecedent of *it* clear to readers. That's the fancy way of saying they don't show to what *it* refers.

- A train whistle blows as it rocks past. (Grammatically, *it* is the whistle that rocks, but I assume she meant the train.)
- Good health begins with daily exercise. Watch for the ways *it* will change you. (What will change you? health or exercise?)

When I use the pronoun *it*,
I'll make the antecedent clear.

Toward/Towards
and Backward/Backwards

*

WITH THE "S" IS BRITISH; AMERICAN IS WITHOUT THE "S." Because of lazy writing, this distinction isn't always made. But you now know the difference and can't plead ignorance.

- She limped towards her bedroom door.
- I remember only one occasion when I showed anger towards a friend.
- *Count backwards from ten before you speak.*

This isn't what I call a serious error, but it's one of those little things that serious, skilled writers try to avoid.

In the same way is the spelling of words such as gray. The Brits use *grey* and Americans write *gray* (unless it's a surname). Except in older poems and hymns, we don't spell labor and *Savior* with a "u," although they still do in the UK (labour and Saviour).

> Because I want to become an excellent writer,
> I know that small things are important.

38

Four Invisible Verbs

*

WHEN WE WRITE DIALOG, most of the time we want readers to focus on *what* the speakers say and not on *how* they say it. To keep the emphasis on the dialog itself, you can use four different verbs—I call them invisible—because they are so common, we hardly notice them. They are *said, ask, answer,* and *reply*.

Please read these two sentences aloud to get the full effect.

"I walked the entire sixteen blocks," Harlan blurted out.

"I walked the entire sixteen blocks," Harlan said.

Did you notice the emphasis? In the first sentence, "blurted out" grabs your attention and you become aware of how Harlan spoke. Nothing wrong if that's what you want readers to get.

> In dialog, when I want the emphasis on what's said, I use one of the *invisible* words of attribution.

Behave Professionally

*

PROFESSIONALS ARE PEOPLE ON WHOM EDITORS DEPEND. If you're a professional, you don't just make your deadlines, you beat them. You're dependable.

Many years ago, I received opportunities to ghostwrite for a publisher—and did a total of 35 for them. I didn't know the reason they asked me to do so many. A decade later, an editor told me that one woman had written many books for them, and she was excellent. They had one problem with her: She failed to meet deadlines. *Every deadline*. They got tired of working with her. They had books on a production schedule and the editorial staff got tired of phoning and waiting.

If you're a professional, you also learn to take criticism well. (It may not be an easy lesson to learn). Remind yourself that you're still a learner and editors want to help you look better. You may need to remind yourself that you'll always, always, always need someone to edit behind you.

Even when you don't agree with what an editor says, seriously ponder it instead of responding with anger. Think of it as two professionals working together to develop one excellent product.

A once-famous writer called an editor on the phone and berated her and the editing of her manuscript. (I heard the account from someone who sat in the editor's office.) The writer yelled and screamed for *nearly five hours*. That may be a big reason she's no longer a famous writer.

I could list other characteristics, but professionals seem to have an innate sense of the correct thing to do at the right time.

Professionals try to be sensitive to others, especially in the way they treat people who are a few rungs lower on the ladder than they are.

I am a professional;
I act like a professional.

Reach Out to Other Writers

*

THIRTY YEARS AGO, SUZANNE REFUSED TO HELP ANOTHER WRITER because "she'll become my competition." I didn't agree then; I strongly disagree today.

I believe in the principle of giving yourself freely, and sharing what you know. Don't think of others as your competition. Consider it an opportunity to help others sell what they write.

To the fearful and insecure, it may sound outrageous to give away what you've worked hard to learn. But it really works the other way. I'm a natural giver and I like to give. As I examine my writing career, every upward step I've taken has come about because someone else opened the door.

My first book publisher and my first agent came because someone else opened the door. In both instances, the help was from individuals I had helped but from whom I never expected anything in return.

Professionals know that. They enjoy sharing what they know and giving to others. That puts them in a position to receive from others.

I receive by giving;
I grow by sharing.

2

* * *

Start to Finish

Is It Necessary
to Write Articles First?

*

I WON'T SAY YOU CAN'T GET A BOOK PUBLISHED without going the article route; I will say that writing articles makes it easier *when you're ready to sell your book.* Here are the advantages:

- You prove that you can start and complete a writing project.
- You prove that you have publishing experience.
- Articles help you gain credibility in the marketplace.
- You can show that you have the skills for a magazine piece.
- You show you can write a specific length to fit the magazines.
- You can handle editing by a professional and rewrite if requested.
- Your publishing credits show that you have begun to establish name recognition.
- If your book is nonfiction, you could write the chapters and sell them as articles. (Sell only first or one-time rights.) You'll reshape them some for a book later, but the bulk of the research and writing will be done.

I don't have to write articles first;
but it's an excellent way to break into publishing.

More Reasons
for Starting with Articles

*

TOO MANY WRITERS WANT TO START WITH A BOOK without proving themselves as writers first. This is a proven strategy for rejection. Writing isn't something we perfect overnight. It takes hard work and dedication.

Geoff Colvin's research for *Talent Is Overrated* urges "deliberate practice—a life-long period of deliberate effort to improve performance in a specific domain."[7] His research refers to the ten-year rule, which states that talented performers don't become great "without at least ten years of very hard preparation," and goes on to add, "...authors produce their greatest work only after twenty or more years of devoted effort."[8]

Think of articles as your apprenticeship. You write and sell articles to learn the craft and to understand the business.

More than 100 of my articles hit print before I started a book. I look back at those experiences as my invaluable apprenticeship. I had to find writing time in the middle of my busy work world and I proved I could do it and meet deadlines. In my diligence to publish, I convinced myself that writing was what I truly wanted to do.

Too many writers don't want to put in the grunt work of learning the rules and applying them. Once I started writing books, however, I knew what I was doing. No matter how well we think we can write, none of us comes into publishing fully developed. We need to master techniques and skills.

Another reason for articles first is that you work for shorter periods of time and get feedback faster. It's easier to handle a rejected article on which you spent three weeks than on a book that took you two years to write and it never sold.

> If I write shorter pieces first, my first book will be superior to what I could have done earlier.

---

[7] *Talent Is Overrated,* Geoff Colvin (New York: Penguin Group, 2008), p. 63.
[8] Op. cit., p. 62.

"I'm a Fiction Writer.
I Don't Do Articles."

*

THAT MAY BE YOUR PROBLEM. If you want to work on short stories, that may be the way to learn the craft, but the market is limited.

Why not start with articles? Even novelists need to know how to construct a chapter—that is, the serious writers realize they need to do more than just write anything that flows through their minds.

Part of learning the craft of writing is to learn the basics. My wife's cardiologist didn't start with his specialty. He studied all the required courses for being an MD. *After that,* he moved into cardiology.

I want to learn to write.
I'm serious enough to start with the foundational principles.

What *Is* a Good Article?

LET'S START WITH A DEFINITION. An article is a short piece that focuses on *one* idea; a chapter is a short piece that focuses on *one* idea. In the chapter of a novel, several things may happen, but the chapter has a single purpose and stays with it. It's just as true with a chapter of a nonfiction book in which you may explain five ways to avoid a heart attack. All five methods stay within the same theme.

Many writers don't understand that simple premise: *Focus on one idea.*

Here's an easy way to see how this works. Pick out two magazines. (I suggest you avoid ezines. Many of them are badly written and poorly edited.) Read three articles in each magazine.

As you read, ask yourself: What is the *one* point the author makes? The title should help. If it's a how-to article called "Three Ways to Lose Weight," that points the direction. If it's something such as "The Day Dad Cried," everything in that piece needs to point to a single, poignant event with no distracting information about where Dad lived when he was fifteen (unless it's relevant) or the fact that he went to school with Brad Pitt's mother's younger brother.

Open a novel at the beginning of any chapter and the principle works. If you look at books from 100 years ago, they often had a table of contents for fiction that told readers what they were about to read in each chapter.

> When I complete an article or chapter,
> I will have focused on *one idea.*

How Do I Write
a Good Article?

*

START WITH PASSION. Find a topic that excites you. Try something simple. Suppose you want readers to manage their time better. Thousands of articles and books have come out on the topic during the past thirty years, so you want to say something that's different.

What unique insight do you have? You could write a personal-experience article on your winning over procrastination and gaining control. You could write a how-to article (which is the most commonly written type). Go back to passion. What grabs you about the topic?

How about starting with something like the Myers-Briggs Personality Types Inventory? It says that you have a *preference* for meeting deadlines (a J in their inventory) or you're a P and you don't get close to meeting deadlines without pressure.

Is the passion stirring? Do the ideas flow? Stay with the manuscript. Ponder the concept. If the J personalities don't need the time-management tips, what do you have to offer the P personalities without inducing guilt?

As you ponder the idea you will do research. What have others said on the topic? At least Google the topic of time management and that can help you learn what's been written on the topic.

If you can write an article infused with passion and can learn to write it well, there is an audience for your ideas.

> I begin an article with a passionate concept.
> That's the best place to start.

What You Know
or What You Yearn to Know

*

LIKE THE REST OF US, YOU LEAD A UNIQUE LIFE. You're a product of your past experiences and no one has a background exactly like yours. Draw from that background. Reflect on what you already know and write it either as fiction, autobiography, how-to, or any other genre you choose. Use your already accumulated knowledge and wisdom (and you probably have more than you think you do).

But don't stop with what you know. Move into what you *want* to know. Research by reading, asking questions, learning about topics that grab your interest. For instance, in 1990 and 1995, I co-wrote two books about Antarctica, even though I didn't visit that frozen continent until 2003.

I read widely because of the two books, the first of which was published by a company that specializes in true adventure and they called it *With Byrd at the Bottom of the World.* It's the story of Norman Vaughan, who was the last surviving member of Richard Byrd's historic flight over the South Pole. (Norman, along with others, disembarked on the icy continent. With a team of men with dog sleds Norman went 400 miles inland while Byrd flew over the true South Pole.)

While working on the two books, I didn't know much about Antarctica, but I read widely and felt as if I had been there long before I boarded a ship at the tip of Argentina to take me there.

That's one of the marks of a professional—they're curious people. That means you want to know more. You refuse to settle for surface information.

I write what I know;
I also find new areas to increase my knowledge.

From Idea to Manuscript

*

1. YOU START WITH *ONE* IDEA—one about which you're passionate. Don't try to write an article just because you think it will sell. You need enthusiasm to stay with it.

2. Decide if there is an audience large enough for your article.

3. Do the research. We all work differently, but be sure you know your topic. If it's a personal-experience piece, be as clear on the facts as possible. Ask others who were involved. Research means you gather information and you also figure out illustrations or anecdotes to make your ideas significant.

4. Start building your ideas around a theme. Everything in your piece needs to point to your central idea. I usually write my concept for articles and for books. It helps me stay focused. For instance, a couple of years ago I worked on something about accountability. Here's my premise: *To whom are you accountable? Most people answer with one word: Nobody.*

Everything in that piece had to keep going back to that statement. I had to show readers they needed someone—a friend, a mentor, or a therapist. That led me to state the benefits of relating to someone else.

5. Write a draft. Leave it for as long as you can—a day or possibly two weeks. I find a week is usually enough for me to get my mind off the topic.

6. Let the unconscious work. That's part of leaving the draft. Try not to think consciously of its strengths or weaknesses.

7. After a time lapse, edit ruthlessly. Take out every weak expression and look for anything that doesn't flow with the topic.

8. You might need to edit more than once. I edited my first article 18 times before I sent it out. (I also sold it to the first magazine to which I sent it.)

9. Send it off. Get it off your desk.

10. Think of a new idea. It's even better if you can think of some other aspect of the topic on which you've written. If you can, you build your credentials *and* those isolated articles become the basis for your book. If not a book, you become an authority on your topic through magazines and ezines.

> Because I want to publish,
> I work systematically and faithfully.

Gather Your Material

*

ONCE YOU KNOW WHAT YOU WANT TO WRITE and you've decided on one idea for the chapter or article, gather the material. That's called doing research.

Learn everything you can to make your manuscript complete and include all essential information. If it's historical or factual material (even if you write fiction) read widely. Find the one or two best sources—preferably the original sources quoted by others.

Always learn more about a topic than you plan to use. Years ago I wrote a scene in a novel that included a woman's visit to a field of pyrethrum, a natural pesticide. By the time I finished my research, I could have easily written 5,000 words on the topic. In the novel, I wrote one paragraph and used 93 words. That's all I needed for the story.

When you research carefully, you provide accurate information. Keep records. Footnote your writing if needed. If you use online sources, verify the information before you quote.

Decide on the anecdotes and illustrations you want to use. Think of those word pictures as windows. If you have only narrative statements, it's like a building with only walls. If you illustrate with research, you create windows for your readers. You enable readers to see inside the structure and they understand your statements.

As a professional,
I learn everything I can about my topic.

Focus Your Article

*

BEFORE YOU WRITE, PLAN WHERE YOU'RE GOING. If you start with a single concept or idea, you decide on a beginning or introduction and bring in evidence to support your point.

If you have a distinct focus—a single idea—that's where you start. I strongly recommend a written outline. It helps you know where you start and becomes like a map to get you to the end.

Once you know you have the material structured, begin with an illustration or a statement that points readers in the direction the next six pages will take. The story can be either negative or positive—its purpose is to bring out the problem you want to resolve in the article. (This holds true with fiction: You start with someone having a problem.)

Ask yourself questions. Answer them in logical order so that each fact or incident naturally leads to the next.

For example (and those two words are a logical transition from the previous paragraph), you want to write about learning to forgive. The most obvious way is to set up the problem—and it can be done in a few words or two paragraphs.

> I can't remember when I began to detest Maynard. Was it in grade school when he played his stupid jokes on me? Was it the time he stole two dollars from my wallet? Or was it when he started dating Gina because he knew I liked her?

Now I have the problem—the obvious next thing is to resolve the issue. I don't like Maynard, but I need to get those angry, bad feelings out of my life and forgive him. How do I forgive?

Move from setup to the logical steps you followed to forgive. Or you can point out that all of us have times we need to learn to forgive. You tell readers the five things (or seven or three) they need to do. Use your story with Maynard to illustrate the steps.

I focus on a problem or situation
and then show how to arrive at a solution.

Slant Your Article

*

YOU CAN WRITE YOUR ARTICLE TWO DIFFERENT WAYS. The common method is to write an article and search for a magazine or ezine to publish it. That often works—but it's not efficient.

A better way is to slant the article to fit the needs of a particular publisher. That's called "knowing your markets."

For instance, I don't like put-down jokes and I decided to write an article on the subject. I aimed it at parents so that they could set the example for their children.

I sent the article to a magazine and their guidelines stated that staff wrote 90 percent of their articles. I had studied the magazine enough to know my article fit their scope and style, so I sent it. Three weeks later an editor wrote to say she liked the article and that it was exactly the kind of material they wanted. (I felt affirmed by that comment.)

The problem was that they didn't see how they could use it for at least a year. "This isn't fair to you," she wrote, "so please feel free to sell it elsewhere. If you have not sold it within six months, please send it back and we'll accept it for publication."

I didn't want to wait. I changed three sentences to focus on adults in general, gave it a new title, and sent it to a different magazine. They bought it and also paid more money than where I sent it first.

In my early days of writing I wouldn't have known how to do that. Despite my changing the slant for a second magazine, the principles of writing articles still hold. I started my article with one basic thought, illustrated my point, told about the harm of put-down jokes, and offered suggestions on how to avoid that type of humor.

Slanting is part of the craft I learn.
It's more work to slant my writing for a specific publication.
It's also a sign of professionalism.

Two Ways to Outline Your Article

*

HERE ARE TWO METHODS, both of which provide a helpful formula. I'm not a formula-type writer, but both methods have proven beneficial to many.

1. The Train Method. (Visualize the old-fashioned freight train with the snowplow, locomotive, boxcars, and caboose.)

- Snowplow or Cowcatcher: You grab attention, carry readers into the article with a quote, anecdote, or question to rouse curiosity and keep them reading.
- Locomotive: Write the theme or purpose that sets the direction and establishes your focus. It's a concise statement of your viewpoint.
- Boxcars: They carry the evidence that supports your premise. This is the heart or substance of the article and you arrange it in logical sequence.
- Caboose: You end the article so that readers feel they are at the end and you didn't merely stop.

2. The Guideposts Method. This is the basic formula used by Guideposts magazine for their articles.

- Hey! You grab attention.
- You! This is the theme or reason the article is important to readers.
- See! You show your viewpoint or purpose. This is the body of the article.
- So? This is your conclusion. You haven't finished until you show readers the relevance of the article to their lives.

> Because I want to learn,
> I seriously ponder the two formulas.

Write the First Draft

*

FOR THE FIRST DRAFT, GO WILD. Don't censor yourself. Vomit on the page. Let it flow. Remind yourself you can always go back and delete. You'll certainly be able to go back and improve.

If your first draft contains paragraphs that don't fit the topic, delete them. However, you may have stumbled on to an idea for a follow-up article.

Write the draft and don't worry about grammar or style. No one has to see the draft but you. You may be one of those logical, analytical writers who think sequentially. Let it flow. If you're the other kind and your mind jumps around and you end up with a first draft of 5,000 words and you need only one-fifth of the material, that's all right. Don't censor yourself.

The too-many words writer needs to learn to cut, cut, cut. I call that the fat writer. By contrast, I call myself a skinny writer (I am thin, but that's not the reason).

As a skinny writer, even when I let it flow, my first draft reads more like an outline than a full article, but I've written my concepts and major thoughts. If you're a skinny writer, you'll have to add details or information to bring readers into your way of thinking.

When I write my first draft, I vomit on the page. I will go back later and clean up the mess.

Turn Off Your Internal Editor

*

SUSAN ASKED, "How do I turn off my internal editor when typing that first draft?"

It takes self-discipline and unrelenting effort, but it's not self-demanding. The more self-demanding I am, the more difficult the task becomes.

I treat myself with respect and I say aloud each time, "Leave me alone until I finish this draft and then you can tear it apart."

I also remind myself that I can (and will) go back and clean up the mess after I've written it. I also remind myself that I would probably never finish if I stopped to make changes.

> I treat my inner editor
> with respect.

Don't Distract Readers

*

LET'S LOOK AGAIN AT READING TWO MAGAZINES. As you focus on each article, here's another question to ask: *Is there anything that distracts me from a single focus?* Less experienced writers tend to provide too much information and thus divert the power of the message.

Once you have a single-focused idea, you can state it in one sentence. Here are examples:

- If you're considering adoption, here are seven things you need to know.
- People see the patient but the caregiver becomes invisible.
- I didn't want to forgive Betty, but Betty forgave me.

> If I can't reduce an article, scene, or chapter into one statement, I probably haven't focused.

Ignore the Manuscript
for a Time

*

MANY WRITERS FEEL EXHILARATED OR RELIEVED when they write the final word and want to get it to the editor or agent. Resist that urge. Look at it again critically and ask yourself, *Does this sentence make sense? Did I explain it thoroughly? Did I over-explain?* [Note: This is the second time I urge you to leave your manuscript for a time, but for different reasons.]

After I close the file on a manuscript and leave it a few days, perhaps as long as a month, when I come back to it, I can always improve it. I use the absolute *always* because I mean without exception.

When I return to the material, I read it with new insight because the material has been churning inside my unconscious mind. (I intentionally put the previous sentence in the passive voice. I could have written: My unconscious mind churned the material, but the emphasis was on the action—churning—and not on the actor—my mind. This is an extra tip.)

I write to get the story written;
I rewrite to improve the quality.

Two Qualities
Every Article or Book Needs

*

THE OBVIOUS QUALITY IS *UNIQUENESS*. What can you say that hasn't been said endlessly and probably better than you could?

One major method I used in my early days is what I call the yes-but concept. When I read what others wrote on a topic in which I'm interested, I mentally argue with them. I read their presentation and say, "Yes, that's true, but…" That is, I try to think of what the author isn't saying or I raise my own questions.

The second quality every article needs is *universality*. Whatever idea you have, you need to show readers how it applies to them. Your premise must be important enough for readers to say, "Yes, that's something I need to read."

If you want to talk about coping with an illness that only one person in 40 million people face, you'll have trouble marketing that idea. But you could write about the mental and physical anguish of coping with a debilitating illness and use your experience to illustrate your premise.

When I write for publication,
I remind myself of uniqueness and universality.
My writing needs both.

Writing How-to Articles

*

WHY WOULD YOU WANT TO WRITE A HOW-TO ARTICLE OR BOOK? The answer is that readers constantly seek for ways to enrich their lives and improve their skills. If you have expertise in any area, you can pass it on to eager learners.

What many call self-help articles or books really fit into this category. You tell people how to do something. It may be how to lose weight, marry a millionaire, build a birdhouse, or read the Bible.

Here are suggestions on how to write how-to pieces.

1. Be sure you have the credentials. That doesn't always mean an earned doctoral degree or being CEO of a large corporation. Sometimes experience is the best credential. Years ago, I sold more than thirty articles on making marriage better. My credentials came from the experience of being happily married.

Here are questions for you to consider:
- What do I know that many others may not?
- What have I learned to do that I can pass on to help readers?
- What am I passionate enough about to make me yearn to tell others?
- Who am I to write on this topic?

That last question may cause you to pull back, but ponder it anyway. Today, publishers want credentials and you'll have to prove you are an expert if you want to write about "What Our Dreams Say About Us." But you might want to write "Five New Approaches to Being a Better Parent."

I once wrote an article on how to listen to sermons. I used simple suggestions and the article was republished 17 times.

You might be surprised how many things you know that others would love to learn. One man, a runner for more than 30 years, wrote a how-to book on what he knew—how to run and not be injured.

If I know how to do something well,
I can write how-to articles or books.

Writing How-to Articles
PART 2 OF 5

*

HERE ARE TWO MORE TIPS about how-to articles (or books):

1. Don't try to cover too much material. Don't tell readers everything you know in one article on how to exercise, how to read the Bible, or how to start a successful online business. About 1,200 words make a good how-to piece (although that varies with publishers), and today you don't want to write more than 2,000.

2. Start with a concept statement. When I start any project, I write the heart of the material in no more than 50 words. Here's my concept statement for an article on how to write how-to articles (even though I send it out in small pieces): Ten suggestions on how to write simple information to help others write how-to manuscripts. (I used 14 words.) Simple, right? If you can't put your concept into less than 50 words, you probably haven't narrowed your focus.

In 2004, I wrote a book called *Committed But Flawed* with the subtitle of *Seeking Fresh Ways to Grow Spiritually.* It's a how-to book, even though my publisher classified it as a devotional guide. Some church groups have used the book for adult Sunday school classes and one church is using it as a men's study.

Here's the concept statement I wrote for that book (with 36 words):

> In his search for spiritual growth, Cecil Murphey studied the committed-but-flawed people in the Bible. Using them as patterns each day in prayer, Murphey envisions himself as the individuals who embody those spiritual qualities he desires.

I write a concept statement for myself
to know exactly what I want to teach.

Writing How-to Articles

*

1. PICK ONE THEME AND FOCUS ON THAT SUBJECT. Even if you want to do an entire book, write each chapter as if it were an article. Make each chapter stand on its own, even when it builds on the previous chapters.

Sometimes that's obvious and here's an example. I expressed the topic for my book *Aging Is an Attitude,* by its subtitle: *Positive Ways to Look at Getting Older.* I wrote the book because I got tired of negative media images and out of my own struggles about getting older. I also realized I couldn't choose to age—God made that decision—but I could decide my attitude during the process.

Every chapter in that book goes back to one point, even if I don't state the words: Here's another positive way to look at getting older.

2. Make your writing straightforward. You're giving information to readers who want to learn something, extend their knowledge, or look at a subject in a different way. Your article could be as straightforward as seven ways to stretch your money in a down economy or how to find thirty minutes (or five or ten) each day for a quiet time with God.

I write how-to articles and books
to give information about how to do something.

Writing How-to Articles

*

HERE'S MORE ON HOW TO WRITE HOW-TO ARTICLES AND BOOKS.

1. Keep the language simple. That's true with any kind of writing, but it's especially true when we try to explain the way to do something.

2. Close to that is making the instructions easy to follow. You want to keep readers moving, not make them stammer or ask, "What do you mean?" Make each point and move on. How-to pieces aren't to impress readers with your knowledge of Sanskrit or your advanced education. Use bullets and lists if they make the material more quickly absorbed.

3. Write in an informal, friendly style. Don't be afraid to address readers as you (as I do in this book). In most writing, the I-we approach works better because it implies, "I'm like you." But when you give instructions, you become the expert and this is how you teach.

4. Keep the word *practical* at the center of your writing. Think of this as explaining something to a neighbor who asks, "How do you...?" Illustrate or clarify points by giving examples, as I do in most of my blogs.

> When I write how-to articles,
> I clearly show readers how to do it.

Writing How-to Articles

*

HERE ARE A FEW MORE SUGGESTIONS.

1. Don't write lengthy, convoluted sentences or long paragraphs. Readers want information—and they want it quickly, so you need to make it easy to grasp. I have a rule about paragraphs. I don't send out anything with more than eight lines to a paragraph (and I usually stay below that).

2. Don't confuse a personal essay with a how-to piece. If your article is about how to teach an adult-education class, don't bog down the material with statements on the importance of teaching. That is implied, because your readers are those who are interested in learning to teach better.

3. Win readers' trust by convincing them you understand their problems. Because you identify with their situation, they feel they can trust you to offer solutions. For example, chapter one of *Aging Is an Attitude* begins: "Getting older used to scare me—and I suspect I'm not alone."

After that initial statement, I've included readers' concerns. I show that I understand their anxieties because I used to feel that way.

> My how-to manuscripts show that I perceive readers' needs.

Don't Forget the Message

*

NONFICTION WRITERS SELDOM HAVE TROUBLE WITH THE MESSAGE—the point, the significance—of the writing. It has a purpose. Fiction writers often miss the point. Every good novel has a message. It can be as simple as "True love wins over deceptive tricks," "The good can sometimes be led astray by ambition," or "Lawbreakers get caught."

The message doesn't have to be obvious to readers, but it needs to be there. People like a good story, but the value they take from the book is the implied message you give them. I enjoyed every volume of the well-written Harry Potter series. I expected the same quality from J.K. Rowlings' *A Casual Vacancy*. I didn't read about one character I liked. No one lived by standards to encourage or challenge me. Maybe her message was that life is boring and meaningless.

I write to entertain,
and I write to impart my views
and my values—my message.

Revise and Polish
Your Article

*

CALL IT EDITING, REVISING, OR POLISHING, it means you work on the article until it's the best you can do.

I wrote 18 full drafts of my first article. After that, I revised each a few times. Perhaps 15 on the second article (I no longer remember). By then, I had gained knowledge on how to write. I continued working to improve.

I still write occasional articles and I go through the same steps, but I write fewer drafts. I rarely go beyond the third. Even on the third, it really is polishing and not editing.

Here are a few hints on polishing your work.

• Look for awkward or laborious sentences.

• Seek ways to cut unneeded words. Get rid of adjectives and adverbs that don't enhance the writing.

• Sharpen your focus (if needed).

• Look at the number of times you use the same word in your article. If you use a word 12 times, that's too many. Look at a thesaurus for synonyms (but don't use one unless you know what it means).

> My article is never good enough
> until it's good enough for me to say,
> "I can't improve it."

Polish Your Writing Again
PART 1 OF 2

*

I LIKE TO REWRITE. Sound crazy? Not to me, because I enjoy finding ways to make my writing better. Below are some of the things I look for when I get into Serious Mode Editing.

I scrutinize for clichés, fuzzy thoughts, grammatical problems, poor word choice, and favorite words I've used too often. I ask myself: *Have I written with a logical progression?* Too many writers touch on a topic and four paragraphs later go back to the same point.

Another thing: I read the final sentence of a paragraph and the first of the next to see if I've made good transitions. If you read the two previous sentences, you'll see that by starting this paragraph with "another thing," I made a transition. You had no trouble following my thoughts.

I get rid of clutter, such as redundancies and laborious phrases. A good rule is that if I can think of a simpler word, I use it in place of a long word. We write to communicate, not to impress.

I check sentence length. When I get above 20 words in a sentence with no commas or semicolons, I've already strained the grasp of some.

I especially look for clichés. I'm weary of reading those overused phrases. At Christmas, for example, I must have read 50 ads that touted the *perfect* Christmas gift. Not only is nothing perfect, but the word has become meaningless.

I've dealt with clichés in another section, but think of it this way: If it's an expression you've heard before, it's probably a cliché. Find a different-but-clear way to say it.

I will revise my manuscript. Then I will do it again.
There is no magic number of revisions,
but it's always more than one.

Polish Your Writing Again

*

YOU'VE EDITED ONCE AND YOU'RE FINISHED.

I doubt it.

Keep editing and revising it until you know you can't make it better.

Look for redundancies. Most writers tend to overwrite and to say the same thing three or four times with different words. In print, you need to say something only once (unless you're using it as a literary device). Therefore, when you polish, aim for brief articles and short chapters.

Today, articles run 800 to 1,800 words and if you stay below 1,200 words, you're probably about right. Chapters have also gotten shorter. For an example, look at the novels of James Patterson. None of his chapters take up more than five pages. Each is one scene, and a decade ago editors would have combined several of them into a single chapter. Patterson caters to the byte-size generation and his books consistently hit the best-seller lists.

> My writing may not hit the best-seller lists,
> but I can make it the best writing I'm capable of producing.
> And if it's my best, that's good enough—*for now.*

Write a Good Query

*

YOU CAN FIND A PLETHORA OF BOOKS AND ARTICLES on how to write a query letter. I suggest you avoid them. I've read some of those supposedly can't-fail ideas and I wouldn't accept any of them. My basic query idea applies whether you write to agents or editors.

Here are two things you need to bear in mind:

- Keep the query brief.
- Make it a professional-looking business letter whether you use paper or email.

I suggest you write *one paragraph* that expresses your idea for a book or an article. Call it the elevator pitch, précis statement, or concept (the term I use). Don't give them a sales pitch such as, "This book will revolutionize the way people eat cereal." State your premise and let them make value judgments.

In the second paragraph tell them about yourself. Give them your background, education, experience, and your work or profession—anything that shows your credentials to write the article or book.

Your next paragraph reads:

May I send you my article? If it's a book, you ask to send your book proposal. If you have completed your manuscript, you write: May I send you my proposal or my completed manuscript?

Query letters are simple sales pitches. Make no claims for what your article or book will do. Just tell them what it *is.*

My query letter is a business letter.
It asks an editor to buy my product,
and the editor probably knows the product better than I do.

Stop. Let Go.

*

WHEN I FINISHED THE EIGHTEENTH DRAFT OF MY FIRST ARTICLE, I knew I couldn't improve it. Today I could, but that was the best I could do then. An editor or someone else might make it better, or in another year I might have developed my skills enough to make it better. But not then.

To myself I said aloud, "This is the best I can do at this stage of my development." I still repeat those words before I send in a manuscript. It's my way to let it go.

Someone told me, "I have to decide if I will release my imperfect manuscript or hold on to the perfect manuscript inside my head."

When I can say,
"This is the best I can do at this stage of my development,"
I give myself permission to stop.

Do I Send the Manuscript
as an Attachment?

*

I HEAR THAT QUESTION FREQUENTLY. Email transmission is now the norm. However, it's your responsibility to find out. If you query an editor (which you will) by email or through the mail, you ask for permission to send your article or your proposal.

Their websites will usually tell you how they want to receive queries and manuscripts. If you're not sure, ask, "Would you prefer I send it as an email attachment or by mail?"

Some editors are so afraid of downloading a virus, they won't open an attachment unless it's from someone they know. Other editors don't want to read new submissions from their screens. They want the hard copy so they can read while eating lunch, riding the subway, or whenever they get free minutes—and there aren't many free minutes. If they have to print your manuscript, you've added to their daily load.

Some editors and agents download manuscripts to their Kindles or iPads. Stay with hard copy unless you know differently. As more editors adapt to the apps on their Smartphones and other electronic equipment, this will probably change.

Assume that editors are overworked (and I don't know any who would say they're not). Make life easier for them. Do it their way.

> If I'm not sure how to send a manuscript,
> I ask.

If You Send Your Manuscript
Through the Mail

*

INSIDE THE ENVELOPE, enclose a self-addressed stamped envelope (SASE) and return postage. (Of course, you will keep a copy of the manuscript on your computer and a safety copy on a CD, flash drive, external hard drive, or an off-site storage such as Carbonite.)

After that, you wait.

And you wait.

And wait.

Never call an editor unless you have permission. Their guidelines will tell you how long it normally takes them to respond. Respect that. Give the editor at least one month beyond their stated time. If you haven't heard after five months, send a letter with SASE and say something like this:

> March 7, 2013
>
> On October 10, 2012, I sent you my article titled, "Beyond the Amateur Look." If you're still interested, please take whatever time you need. If you're not interested, please return my manuscript.
>
> I've enclosed SASE for your convenience. (If you send the query by email, ask for a response in the same way.)

If it has been a reasonable amount of time with no word from the editor, this is the professional way to find out the status of your manuscript.

None of this information guarantees you'll get published. It does assure you that you'll look professional and editors will assume you're not a beginner. That's a good start, isn't it?

Conforming to professional standards is never wrong, and it may help me get published.

One More Thing
You Need to Do

GOOD WRITERS ARE NEVER SATISFIED WITH THEIR WRITING. They know they can improve even though they're not sure how. So they continue learning and reading about writing.

Each morning I spend about ten minutes online reading blogs for writers, trying to glean insight. Many of them are helpful. The more I grow as a writer, the more aware I become of good writing and weak writing.

I also read widely—far, far outside the fields in which I write. I promised myself and God that I would never stop learning. In that commitment I promised that I would read at least one book a week. (I'm about 10 years ahead of my proposed number.)

> I want to be known as a growing writer.
> I can be known that way if I remain a learner.
> I promise myself not to stop learning.

The Rules Differ with Books

*

1. IF YOU'RE WRITING A BOOK, use a cover sheet and write your title and byline halfway down the page. Follow that with the genre, such as: Historical Fiction of 80,000 words; Autobiography of 70,000 words.

Most editors and agents tell you to put in the number of words. If you do, round them off. Don't write 78,349 words but "about 80,000 words." It's an approximation and by the time your manuscript has been accepted and edited, it may run only 70,000 or 85,000.

Although I'm supposed to tell you to give your word count, I don't. My reasoning is that if the publisher wants only 50,000 and you have 85,000, that's a good reason to reject you. If they turn you down, let it be for a different reason.

2. At the bottom of the cover page, centered or at the far left, list your name, address, email address, and phone number. It would look like this:

My name
Street address
Email address
Phone number

If an agent represents you, you don't list your personal information. Instead write "Represented by" and give the agent's contact information.

3. On the next page, start one-third of the way down the page for the first chapter or introduction. Every chapter begins a third of the way down the page. *Don't renumber pages for each chapter.*

4. Don't send the manuscript unless you have permission. Query first.

Looking professional
is an important aspect of my *being* professional.

3

* * *

Show Me. Show Me.

What Do We Mean
by "Show and Not Tell"?

*

THE FIRST MAJOR PIECE OF ADVICE hurled at beginning writers is, "Show, don't tell." I prefer to say, "Whenever possible, show readers." If writers do nothing but show, their articles and books go on endlessly.

What do we mean by *show?* Think of this principle as presenting a picture—something readers can see if they close their eyes. Good showing also involves other senses, but it's easier to show this using the visual.

Here's an example: I jogged through a San Francisco neighborhood. That sentence told you facts. If you can close your eyes and capture a scene, it's because you have read something into the text that wasn't there.

By contrast, here's the way James Patterson wrote it: "I jogged past yelping dogs running loose, lovers on a morning walk, gray-clad, bald-headed Chinese men bickering over mah-jongg."[9]

Patterson uses two senses and we see the dogs, the lovers, the Chinese, and we *hear* the dogs as well as the bickering.

That's good writing, because he drew a picture for us and pulled us into the San Francisco scene. In one sentence, we jog alongside the protagonist and live vicariously.

Good writing is subtle.
I can insert one simple detail
and it conveys more than a paragraph of telling statements.

---

[9] *First to Die,* James Patterson (Little, Brown, 2001), p. 104.

You Can Learn to Show

*

HERE'S WHAT WE CALL A TELLING STATEMENT: Jason raged against his wife. Because *rage* is a strong verb, many writers assume they've shown emotion. They haven't.

Here's a picture of rage: Jason grabbed Ellen's chiffon dress off the hanger and ripped it down the front. He threw it to the floor and stomped on it with his muddy boots.

You may think the art of showing is a modern concept, but it's long been the mark of good writing. Here's an example from the 1857 novel *Madame Bovary*. If Gustave Flaubert had been a lazy writer, he could have said, "Charles Bovary was a boring person." Despite the piece being a trifle long, he makes us see and feel Charles:

> Charles's conversation was as flat as a sidewalk, with everyone's ideas walking through in ordinary dress, arousing neither emotion, nor laughter, nor dreams. He had never been curious, he said, to go and see a touring company of Paris actors at the theatre. He couldn't swim, fence, or shoot, and once he couldn't even explain to Emma a term about horseback riding she had come across in a novel.[10]

I show because it brings life to my writing and makes readers feel they're part of my story.

---

[10] *Madame Bovary*, Gustave Flaubert (CreateSpace, 2011), p. 60.

Why Do You Need to Show?

*

TELLING IS LIKE OVERHEARING SOMEONE TALK about another person; showing is like being introduced to the person. Showing allows readers to draw inferences and evaluate the action; it involves them emotionally and they become part of the story. The rule applies to nonfiction or fiction.

If you say, "Evelyn had a broken leg," readers can't feel anything, but if you describe a bare bone sticking through pale skin or describe the way she hobbles on crutches, they vicariously experience Evelyn's injury.

This is especially important in dealing with the emotional state. Don't say a person is depressed; readers need to see the person acting in a depressed manner. It's the adage that actions speak louder than words—especially *telling* words. When done well, showing reveals character and enables readers to feel they are participants in the events.

Suppose I relate an incident when I arrived late for my English class. Before I write, however, I need to decide what information and emotion I want to convey to my readers. Notice the differences in these three examples:

1. I *walked* into Miss Anderson's classroom five minutes late. (This presents information without emotions.)

2. I *raced* into Miss Anderson's classroom, desperately hoping she wouldn't see that I was late. (Readers can visualize this.)

3. I *sneaked* into Miss Anderson's classroom as the clock ticked again. I cringed to realize that I was five minutes late. (This enables readers to feel my emotions.)

No matter how small the action, don't merely inform. The examples above shows how much life you can add to a sentence by the use of a few words.

You could make the illustration even stronger:

4. I sneaked into Miss Anderson's classroom, desperately hoping she wouldn't see that I was five minutes late. My pulse raced as I tiptoed to my desk. Just then my book crashed to the floor and heads turned toward me. Miss Anderson's dark eyes glared.

Ask yourself:
When I show, what do I want readers to feel?

What Are the Benefits of Showing?

*

SHOWING:
- enhances reader identification—they're transported into the action;
- provides a sense of time and place, particularly if the story is set in an unfamiliar world;
- creates suspense;
- reveals relationships better than telling;
- offers unique or unusual details and develops feelings of depth and reality;
- hints at or reveals motives behind an action.

This doesn't mean you want to fill the pages with details. Think of capturing an image. Ask yourself, *What is the picture I want to capture?*

A showing exercise. Here's something to consider. Below is a list of common nouns. If you color in details, you give readers a vivid picture. A few, well-chosen details make your fiction or nonfiction come alive.

If I tell you that I met the financial guru Warren Buffett and noticed his wristwatch, what picture have I captured? Nothing special, but if I comment that he wears a Timex, a Seiko, or a Rolex, I'm enlarging the picture. (And, yes, it's all right to use brand names provided you spell them correctly.)

Try this exercise.

Instead of...use:
- a tree...elms, oaks, mesquite, or refer to the golden leaves of the maple.
- a soft drink...name it, but describe your pleasure or disgust as you sip or guzzle.

What would you do to make the following visual?
- a car
- a running shoe
- breakfast

By adding the right details, I open readers' understanding and enable them to sense what I see and feel.

Use Only a Fraction
of What You Know

CHOOSE THE DETAILS YOU WANT READERS TO GRASP. Focus on where the action is or where the drama lies. Go for the emotions and develop a sense of identity. Select elements that allow for an accurate vision and include only the aspects that matter—details that *suggest* more than they describe.

Here's how it works. Ella was sad that Eric was leaving. As she watched him go, she began to cry. The two sentences aren't awful, but the writer hides—that is, readers get no emotional tug.

Here is a showing of the same scene where readers can identify:

Ella waved good-bye from the bedroom window. The first tears slid gracefully down her cheek.

That's not much, but it's enough to make readers care.

Some writers go too far and present a heavy, over-the-top picture, like the following: Tears streamed down Ella's face, nearly blinding her. For nine hours and twenty minutes she wailed over his leaving her for another woman, but no peace came to her. She clutched his door key to her breast and caressed it as her piteous sobs echoed through the empty house.

> "You don't write about the horrors of war.
> No. You write about a kid's burnt socks lying in the road."
> —RICHARD PRICE

Use Telling Statements
for Brief Explanations

*

IF YOUR STORY MOVES ALONG, and you introduce an unfamiliar element to readers, you can interject a one- or two-sentence explanation and move on.

I once wrote a children's novel called *Happy Face* that took place in colonial Kenya, East Africa. Part of my purpose was to show the importance for westerners to learn about the culture. In one scene, Cora, the wife of a rookie doctor, entertains Oko, an African boy.

"Would you like tea?"

He shakes his head. *The white woman has violated tribal custom. If she asks, it means she does not wish to give.*

"I make it with nutmeg," Cora says as she stirs her milk-and-spice tea. "You're sure you don't want some?"

Again, Oko shakes his head and watches. *The aroma of the tea fills the kitchen. He looks away. He cannot tell her he likes the smell of nutmeg better than anything except cinnamon.*

In the middle of that scene, I injected a few sentences of pure telling (italicized above). I could have used dialog. My purpose was not to have Oko correct Cora, but to explain to readers—using telling statements—that the white woman was an ignorant foreigner in an African culture.

I can insert telling information
to help readers grasp information quickly.

Telling Statements
Can Break Down Long Speeches

*

WHY PUNISH READERS by forcing them to read paragraphs of dialog that diminish the drama? Long speeches flatten the writing because they set aside the story's impact too long.

To illustrate how to break up a lengthy passage, let's say Michael Silva, who has won the nomination for mayor, makes his speech before an outdoor audience.

> "You have chosen me to represent you. You have empowered me to speak for those who have no power. I am ready to make our singular voice heard!"
>
> For seventeen minutes, Michael held the crowd's attention. He outlined his plan to "roust the fat cats," get rid of porno websites, declare war on drugs, and bring integrity back to city hall.
>
> "And if you elect me as mayor," he concluded, as he raised his right hand, "you have my solemn word that I will give my total energy to this task."

In writing that scene, I could have cut the lengthy message in several ways. Supporters could have cried out, "That's right!" or, "Right on!" Perhaps even injected the comments by a few hecklers. Michael's gaze could have surveyed the crowd. I could have pointed to the darkening clouds overhead or perhaps had the sun glare in his eyes.

Instead, I chose to insert the telling statement that says he spoke for seventeen minutes. I summarized his message and kept the momentum going.

It is okay to tell—sometimes.
I am learning when to tell and when to show.

Use Telling Statements
to Make Value Judgments

*

IN WRITING, THE MOST IMPORTANT PRINCIPLE we teach, preach, urge, implore, and beg is simple: "Show it." However, it's all right to tell—sometimes. In fact, good writing flows between showing and telling.

When do we tell?

Maybe an example will help. I read an article in *Publisher's Weekly* that was informative and relevant.

Read that last sentence again. That's an example of telling. I stated how I responded to one article. That is, I told readers how to think by citing two positive qualities. I made a simple declarative statement, but I wrote it as an indisputable (and unproven) fact. That defines telling—thinking for readers. At times, that's acceptable and occasionally necessary.

Because good writing is subtle,
I learn to move between showing and telling readers.

Use Telling Statements
to Sum-up Information

*

TELLING SPEEDS UP THE PACE when you don't want to add another ten paragraphs. For instance, I'm throwing us into the middle of a conversation between Reba and her husband, Jerry. He insists she needs to buy a new winter coat.

"This one is good for another year," she said.
"Nobody wears those shapeless, beltless coats anymore. And the color—"
"But I like oracle purple."
"Oceanside blue is the in-color this year."
"We can't afford it. We owe—"
"You need a new coat, and I want you to look good when we attend those holiday events."

They argue about the purchase of a coat. If done right, and without the writer telling us, readers become aware that the argument isn't about buying a coat, but about the way each perceives money: Jerry's a spendthrift; Reba's frugal. After three pages of dialog as well as show-don't-tell writing, readers also grasp that Jerry is the overpowering personality.

Do you need another three paragraphs to show that Reba buys a coat? Probably not. Let's say that's not crucial to the story. So how do you end the scene?

Here's a simple remedy through a telling statement:

Exhausted after the third argument that week, Reba went to Macy's and bought herself a belted oceanside blue coat.

That's called a summary statement.

Sometimes summary statements make good sense.
I won't be afraid to use them.

Use Telling Statements
for Minor-but-vital Information

*

YOU WANT TO BRING READERS up to the present without interfering with the pace.

Suppose Eleanor flies to Europe to seek the proper setting for her new historical novel. You want to let readers know she went to three different places and the fourth one is where the action picks up.

A simple paragraph can bridge the time from her leaving the United States to the moment of action:

> Seven hours after landing at Charles de Gaulle Airport, Eleanor reached the Normandy Coast. After a fruitless day, she left for Zurich where she spent two days. Her Eurail pass took her to Berlin and finally to Brussels.

You need that paragraph of information to authenticate Eleanor's travels. Because nothing dramatic happens until she reaches Brussels, you can leave out three minor scenes. Don't take her through customs or have her struggle with French. Readers don't care. They want her to get to Brussels so the story moves.

I spare my readers from details
they don't need to know.

4

* * *

Working with Verbs

Prefer the Active Voice

*

THAT'S THE RULE: *PREFER*. To use the passive voice isn't a grave trespass even though some writers would rather be strangled with a comma splice than use anything but the active voice. It's easier to slavishly impose a rule than it is to express exactly what you mean. Good writing communicates—that's what you want to keep in mind. That means rules bow to good presentation.

When do you use the active voice?

1. Use the active voice when you want to name the person who does the action. Compare these two sentences.

a. The glass was broken by the baseball.

b. Marty hit the ball that broke the window.

If you want readers to know the culprit, use the second sentence.

2. Use the active voice when you want to speed up the action.

a. The paper was written by Paul, copied by Marla, and presented by Eldon.

b. Paul wrote the paper, Marla copied it, and Eldon presented it.

3. Use the active voice to write shorter sentences. The first sentence below uses nine words and the second only seven. That's not a significant difference in one sentence, but in a book of 500 pages, we might save the life of one tree.

a. The vegetarian meals were eaten eagerly by the visitors.

b. The visitors eagerly ate the vegetarian meals.

Read the partial sentences below. The passive voice shows itself by the use of what we commonly call the helping verb (is, was) and is usually written in the past tense.

- After my arraignment, I was transferred to a cell.
- All my basic needs were taken care of.
- It can be explained only by Pasquale's ignorance.
- Secret knocks are given and tested.
- Her hours were filled with reading and dozing by the fire.
- Invisible boundaries were crossed, but he was unaware.

> Because I want my writing to be strong,
> I choose the active voice.

Avoid the Passive Voice

*

"I HAVE BEEN HONORED BY YOU because I have been given this award." The previous sentence, although grammatically correct, sounds stilted. Twice I used the passive voice with "have been honored" and "have been given."

I'll flip it around and write the sentence in the active voice: "You have honored me because you gave me this award." Both examples are grammatical and we have no problem understanding either, but the second is clearer, stronger, more direct, and uses less words. That classifies itself as better writing.

We call this the principle: Prefer the active, avoid the passive.

Beginning writers often don't grasp the importance of this principle. "It reads fine either way," they say. Sometimes they insist, "The passive voice sounds better." They mistakenly assume that the passive voice lends their work authority, perhaps even an elegant quality. In reality, the passive voice sounds pompous or limp. Why not strive for directness and clarity by using as few words as possible?

I want to be clear on the difference. *Active* refers to someone doing things as opposed to events simply occurring. "Irene delivered the package to Melvin the next morning," compared to, "The package was delivered to Melvin the next morning." Below, not only is the active voice stronger, but the passive voice requires two extra words.

Arlene was infuriated by his behavior. (Passive)

His behavior infuriated Arlene. (Active)

The active voice is stronger and I remember that while I write.

There Are No Passive Verbs

*

CALL ME A CURMUDGEON, but I hate it when people speak of passive verbs. English verbs have voice (active and passive) tense (present, past, and future) and mood (active, passive, and subjunctive, which express wishes or things contrary to fact).

There are no passive verbs.

Here are a few sentences where writers used the passive voice and could make it stronger with the active.

- I'm sorry my essay was poorly written. (If you're going to apologize, apologize: I'm sorry I wrote a bad essay.)
- It has been found regrettable that many families lost their homes during the recession. (This is pompous prose. Try: I'm sorry that many families lost their homes during the recession.)
- Chores were not finished. (This dilutes the apology and hedges on the matter of guilt. Isn't it stronger to write: We didn't finish our chores?)

You need to ask, "Does the subject of the sentence do anything or is something done to it?"

When I write in the passive voice, I weaken the impact and tend to lose the visual image I yearn to create.

Don't Confuse State-of-being Verbs

*

STATE-OF-BEING VERBS include *am, is, are, to be,* and *being.* They are not the passive voice. Consider the difference between "I write" (action verb), "I was being taught to write" (passive voice), and "I *am* a writer" (active voice with verb of being). Most of the time, the *being* verbs become invisible. If you refuse to use them, your writing sounds bloated and overwritten.

Sometimes you want to emphasize the state of being: *The grass was green.* That's an acceptable sentence if you want to emphasize the "is-ness" of grass. You could say the grass grows green, which is trite, but if it grows purple, I'd like to know.

You could overwrite and say the grass stretches from the ground. (Would it come from the sky?) You might try something creative such as: Blades of grass wriggle across the once-barren fields. (Don't they stay in one place?)

If using a strong verb causes you to blink (Huh? What does that mean?), change it. *The grass was green* makes sense and our eyes pass on quickly. Careful use of state-of-being words is acceptable. (Did you notice the state-of-being verb in the previous sentence?)

> State-of-being verbs are useful in my writing
> and that's why they're part of the language.

You Can Avoid
the Passive Voice

*

READ ALOUD FROM A HARD COPY OF YOUR MANUSCRIPT. Whenever you spot a passive verb or a state-of-being verb, circle it in red. That will help you trap those weak verbs and passive statements. Then rewrite the sentence.

You can set most computers to flag passive verbs. (In Word, it's under Tools.)

Do a global search for particular words. For example, passive words need a helping verb such as *was* or *had*. Don't feel you must delete every use. Ask yourself, "Does this work? Is this what I want to say?" (I used *is* in that sentence.)

It may demand time and energy to get rid of the passive voice, but I take pride in my work and prefer the active voice.

When Do You Use
the Passive Voice?

*

SOME WRITERS EQUATE USING THE PASSIVE VOICE with something like picking their noses in public. Here's the principle in one sentence: *When you don't know who did something or you don't want readers to know, use the passive voice.*

- *Use* the passive when you want to de-emphasize the doer. That is, the thing acted on is more important than the actor. The clothes were received by the two grateful refugees. Who gave them isn't important in this instance.

- *Use* the passive when you want to command or give your words authority. *Smoking is not permitted in this building* is stronger (and less argumentative) than *you may not smoke in this building*.

- Sometimes the person doing something isn't significant and you want to emphasize the action. Twila Belk was arrested at noon yesterday. Who arrested her may not be important.

- *Use* the passive when you want to prepare for the punch line: The gold medal in the triathlon competition was won by a ten-year-old girl. This withholds the information until the end of the sentence.

- *Use* the passive when you want to achieve a rhythm and the cadence determines the style. Someone pointed this out to me: Robert Frost could have written, "I took the road where not many people traveled," but who would dispute the cadence of "I took the road less traveled by"?

It's not a felony to use the passive voice,
but it's a serious misdemeanor
when I avoid it because I'm afraid of breaking a rule.

More on the Active
vs. the Passive Voice

*

SOME WRITERS GET SO CAUGHT UP in avoiding the passive voice that they refuse to use state-of-being verbs such as *is* and *was*. In a large writers conference, one prominent writer on a panel yelled, "I hate *to be* verbs."

She misunderstood to-be verbs and assumed they were only helping verbs (copula) in the passive voice.

State-of-being verbs are *not* the passive voice, although they are weak. I can think of no more natural way to write the following sentence: Even though it is December, dandelions are on my lawn. (Yes, I used *two* state-of-being verbs.) I could have written, Even though December had arrived... That's where personal preference comes into writing. In the second instance about dandelions, I could have used an active verb: cover my lawn or invaded. As written, however, *dandelions are on my lawn* causes no problems to understand. It's brief and describes the status of the lawn.

> I sometimes use state-of-being verbs,
> but I'm aware of their purpose.
> I distinguish them from the passive voice.

Be Cautious about
Writing in the Present Tense

*

AVOID WRITING IN THE PRESENT TENSE. It is *not* wrong and several famous contemporary authors use that style. Those who use the present tense usually do so by writing in first person.

I suggest not using the present tense because it's not natural to the written word. Historically, we have written our articles and books in the past tense. It's an adjustment to the brain to shift to present tense.

The present tense makes the writing sound as if it is happening right now: I walk into the room and stare at the ornate surroundings. I move across the room and smile at Thelma.

This present-tense style has become popular in Young Adult (YA) fiction. If written well, readers relate to the voice of the character by living and following each step of the protagonist's venture and self-discovery. One author said, "Readers stand next to the main character and open up as the character develops."

Present tense means readers learn only what the protagonist does and as those actions occur. They're thrilled, surprised, or touched by the poignancy. One avid reader of present tense gushed, "Present tense sounds more genuine. It's a form of self-reflection. I become that person and experience what he does."

Despite the advocates, writing in the present tense is difficult and most writers who try it don't have the skills to make it believable. You have to work hard to stay in the present and not allow your prose to sneak back into the past.

Unless I have a compelling reason,
I write in the normal, past tense.

What Is the Subjunctive Mood?

*

"IF I WERE YOU, I'd write a novel," Harold said.

"No, no," he scolded. "If I *was* you. I is singular."

"Yes, but I am not you," Harold answered. "The statement is contrary to fact, so you use the subjunctive mood."

"The what?" he asked.

Even though you probably use it frequently, you're likely unaware of it. The almost-obsolete subjunctive mood lurks in our language, and careful writers respect it. Please notice, we call it a mood; it is not a tense or voice, such as active or passive.

You don't need to memorize this, but English has three moods: *indicative, imperative,* and *subjunctive.* The indicative mood makes statements and asks questions; the imperative mood commands or requests; the subjunctive expresses wishes, desires, requirements, or conditions.

We've all heard people say (and it's correct):
- Whether it be
- Far be it from me
- As it were
- I wish you were

The following sentences use the subjunctive mood correctly:
- If she *were* rich, would she be kind?
- Unless the weather *were* to change, we'll have our annual picnic.
- "If music *be* the food of love, play on" (William Shakespeare, *Twelfth Night).*
- "If I *were* two-faced, would I be wearing this one?" Abraham Lincoln once said.
- He yelled *as if* the house were on fire.

> If the clause begins with *as if* or *although,*
> I usually need the subjunctive mood.

96

Conditional Sentences

*

WE CAN WRITE CONDITIONAL SENTENCES (usually beginning with *if*) two ways. *If the clause starts the sentence,* put a comma after the statement. In the previous sentence, I gave you the example.

You don't need a comma *if you end the sentence with a conditional clause.* This is the second method. Ending with the conditional clause doesn't seem to cause problems.

> If I begin a sentence with *if,*
> I'll put a comma after the end of the clause or phrase.

Use the Past Tense
and Past Perfect Properly

*

THERE ARE TWO USES FOR THE PAST PERFECT TENSE. They require a form of the verb *has* before the verb, which is the easy way to recognize their use. We often use clue words such as *after*. After I had eaten breakfast, I went for a walk.

Past perfect shows action finished or completed in the past. What we call the simple past tense means anything that took place before the present moment—even four seconds ago. Writers don't seem to have trouble with simple past. Past perfect, however, means action finished in the more distant past (even if it happened three minutes ago).

Here are examples:

- *I had wanted to study at Yale.* That sentence means that in the past I wanted to study at Yale, but it's no longer my desire.
- Esther was married to Joe, but now she's single. That seems obvious. You go from the simple past (what she was) to the is-ness of the present.
- Esther had been married to Joe, but she divorced him, is now single, and will marry Patrick. In that sentence we show the distant past, the more recent past, the present, and the future.

Past perfect also shows which previous action took place first.

- I visited Africa because I had once lived there.
- I had wanted silence, but I settled for soft noises.

I remind myself that the past perfect tense means action done before the immediate past.

Avoid the Progressive Tense

*

CAREFUL WRITERS AVOID THE PROGRESSIVE TENSE because it requires more words and it's less precise. For example, I will be teaching next month in Los Angeles. The simple future works better and is clear: I will teach next month. The progressive tense is usually awkward and implies that I am even now in the process of teaching next month.

The progressive tense isn't grammatically wrong, but it becomes what we call lazy or imprecise writing. If we think *in the process of,* we'll probably use the tense well. It means some action is ongoing and uses a participle (an active verb with an –ing ending).

It's correct to use the progressive tense to express frequent action: We will be going to church Sunday. But it's just as easy to use the future tense: We will go to church Sunday.

Present progressive tense indicates an action that takes place right now. It uses a "to be" verb and the present participle:
- I am walking to the store.
- He is lecturing to the class.

Use the simple past:
- I walked to the store.
- He lectured to the class.

Indifferent writers use the present progressive for future action.
- My brother is graduating next month.
- I will be visiting Canada in September.

Careful writers prefer the future tense:
- My brother will graduate next month.
- I will visit Canada in September.

Because I am a careful writer,
I avoid using the present progressive tense.

Avoid the Past Progressive Tense

*

THIS TENSE REFERS TO AN ACTION that took place in the past and is formed with a "to be" verb and the past participle.

- I was eating lunch with my friends.
- I was writing my monthly newsletter.
- Jane was celebrating her birthday.

The past-progressive form implies an interruption to the action. The implication is that an action began in the past and was left unfinished. For example:

- While I was eating my lunch, the phone rang. That means, I was *in the process of eating* and something interrupted.
- Jane was celebrating her birthday when the lights flickered and went out.

The weakness of using the past progressive tense becomes obvious when you use the passive-progressive form. Compare:

- She was being robbed on Main Street. (That construction implies that someone interrupted the in-progress robbery.)
- She was robbed on Main Street. (The crime was committed and the culprit vanished.)

I make my meaning clear by using simple past, present, and future tenses.

Fun with the Progressive Tense

*

MY FRIEND FRANK BALL WROTE A CLEVER PIECE about the use of the progressive tense. With his permission I'm printing it.

The King of Ing, Rough Draft

At dawn, the King of Ing was standing at his window, wishing for a better way of communicating with his people who were not responding to his commanding style but were sitting, resting, and accomplishing little. He started pacing, moving from one side of the room to the other, contemplating what to do. Knowing improvement was not happening without something changing, he was considering acquiring a differing way of writing. Therefore, using his own quill, he began composing an edict for posting at the city square.

The King of Ing, Revised

At dawn, the King of Ing stood at his window and wished for a better way to communicate with his people who had not responded to his commands but sat, rested, and accomplished little. As he paced from one side of the room to the other, he contemplated what to do. Without change, improvement is impossible, so he considered a different way to write. Therefore, he used his own quill to compose this edict posted at the city square: Your leader has decided to speak in better style as your new Prince of Simple Past Tense.[11]

If I want to amuse or show imprecise writing, I'll use the progressive tense at least once in every paragraph.

---

[11] Frank Ball, founder of North Texas Christian Writers, http://www.helpmetellmystory.com/?page_id=192.

5

* * *

Grammar Rules

Get Rid of the Comma Splice

*

THE TERM *COMMA SPLICE* means that writers join (splice together) two complete thoughts that have no connection. Here is an example: Most of my classmates drink coffee, and caffeine keeps me awake. We know coffee contains caffeine, but there is no connection between the two statements.

- Windows are open to the warm morning air, the air conditioning units are off. To make good sense, you connect them to each other with more than a comma: Windows are open to the warm morning air, because the air conditioning units are off. *Because* joins the two thoughts.
- Most unindustrialized nations have high birth rates, most of their citizens are young. This would work if we wrote, Most unindustrialized nations have high birth rates and, therefore, most of their citizens are young.

Careful writers avoid joining two unconnected thoughts with only a comma.

Avoid the Run-on, Run-together, or Fused Sentence

*

ALTHOUGH SIMILAR TO THE COMMA SPLICE, these independent statements have no commas and thus they run together without any punctuation to indicate where the first ends and the second begins. Here's an example: The great white shark eats humans research shows that most sharks spit them back out. What is humans research? I'd insert a period or a semicolon after humans. Or add a conjunction: ...eats humans, although research...

Edgar Allan Poe is one of America's foremost poets he died in poverty. If you insert a comma and a conjunction, you've made the statement easily understood.

Careful writers avoid run-on or fused sentences by adding commas or conjunctions.

Serial Commas

*

MOST BOOK PUBLISHERS differ from newspapers and magazine publishers in the use of what we call the serial comma. For books you write, I gave the money to Mary, Thomas, and Philip. That is, a comma before the conjunction *and*. In magazine articles, you omit the comma before the conjunction so that it reads, Mary, Thomas and Philip.

Book publishers use the *Chicago Manual of Style (CMS* or *CMOS)*, which has been around since 1906 and is updated irregularly. The 16th edition came out in 2010. Most magazines, ezines, and newspapers use the *Associated Press Style Guide (AP)*, which is updated annually.

Notice the difference in the two styles: He bought spaghetti sauce, noodles and a package of brownie mix. (The *CMOS* would insert a comma after noodles.) He peeled back the lid, snared a wing and offered it to Cynthia. Again, the CMOS would put a comma after wing.

• Both of them are angry, hurt and eager to fight.

Think clarity first. Sometimes even the AP inserts a comma before the conjunction. The classic example goes like this: He willed his estate to Tom, Mary and Jim. Without the comma following Mary, it means Tom receives half while Mary and Jim share the other 50 percent. If the author intends it to be divided into thirds, it would read: ...Tom, Mary, and Jim.

My suggestion: Insert the comma before the final conjunction. If a publisher doesn't use what we call the serial comma, your editor can easily remove it.

> When I write for clarity,
> I use the serial comma.

Avoid Faulty Parallelism

*

FAULTY PARALLELISM HAPPENS when you put words in a series and they don't match (or aren't parallel to) the grammatical structure.

For example: Marlene ate chili, chicken, peas, and sliced her bananas. The last item, sliced her bananas, isn't parallel.

You can correct it this way: Marlene ate chili, chicken, peas, and bananas. Or you could write, Marlene ate chili, chicken, and peas. After that, she sliced and ate her bananas.

When I write a series of words, each word will match the grammatical structure.

Was That Meant Parenthetically?

*

WHEN YOU USE PARENTHETICAL EXPRESSIONS CORRECTLY, the sentences make sense and still convey the information you want. They include explanations, digressions, and examples that, although helpful or interesting, aren't essential for the meaning of the sentence. Did you notice my parenthetical expression in the previous sentence?

Your purpose will decide which one you use.

Use parenthetical expressions to include information that *isn't* vital for the intended meaning.

Was That Meant Parenthetically?

*

MY PREFERENCE IS TO USE *THE DASH* when I want to state something significant and it acts more like an interruptive element than a parenthesis. I use *parenthetic marks* more like a way to say "and by the way."

Although the dash has largely deposed the parenthetical expression, they are not the same. The dash signals an added or interrupting thought. The parenthesis (with interesting information) contains less important information while the dash *emphasizes* the addition. The dash (composed of two typed hyphens and no spaces before or after) has become a strong punctuation mark with most commercial writers and has largely replaced the parenthetical marks. If you're in doubt, setting off the expressions with commas works well.

- Martin finally arrived—disheveled and drunk.
- During her entire life—99 years—Anna never tasted alcohol or ate pork.
- His autobiography—if you choose to glorify it with that word—came out in print in 2011.
- The White Sox have a good chance to win the pennant—if they can beat the Orioles.

The dash, however, seems to have become the most overused mark of punctuation. Use it sparingly and it's effective; use it too often and it makes the writing trite or overwritten.

Consider this example of overuse: After we looked for poor Mitsie—for at least an hour—we found her—shivering in the rain. We carried her into the house—really the back porch—and wrapped her in a thick, woolen blanket—an older one that we could throw away.

> The dash interrupts a thought for emphasis.
> I'll use it carefully.

Was That Meant Parenthetically?

*

THE PARENTHESIS HAS LARGELY DISAPPEARED from informal, commercial writing. Remember that parentheses always come in pairs—before and after the punctuated material. I consider the *comma* as more benign than the dash or the parenthesis. With commas, the information is there, but it means it's not particularly significant.

Besides parentheses, we also use commas to set up parenthetical statements, transitional expressions, and mild interjections.

- His research indicates, surprisingly, that caffeine has healthy qualities.
- He tells his story chronologically, except the account of his accident.
- A severe frost, quite late for May, wiped out the spring crop.

Here is where the intention of the writer makes the difference. In the examples above, I could have substituted dashes had I wanted to stress the interruptive elements. I decided that I didn't want to put the emphasis on the parenthetical expressions. The first sentence could have read: His research indicates—surprisingly—that caffeine has healthy qualities.

Parenthetical expressions, set off by commas, are "asides," and add interesting-but-not-vital information.

Using the Ellipsis and Brackets

*

THE ELLIPSIS HAS TWO FUNCTIONS. First, it's used *in quoted material* to shorten the material. You indicate that you have deleted words you consider unimportant for the point you wish to make.

We used to write the ellipsis using three periods without spaces, and some publishers (such as the publisher of this book) still do, but many in the industry put a space between each period. Whatever way you choose, be consistent in your manuscript.

You use a four-period ellipsis at the end of a sentence. The ellipsis is still three periods and the fourth is the end of the sentence. Think of it as a period followed by an ellipsis.

- Butler's report stated, "We will run out of...fossil fuels in thirty-five more years." This sentence indicates words left out of the statement.
- "Comfort the discouraged.... Be patient with everyone" (1 Thessalonians 5:14, COMMON ENGLISH BIBLE). The first period is to show the end of the sentence.

The second use of the ellipsis, as shown below, is to indicate a pause or hesitation.

- What I mean to say is...I don't want to think about it.
- His father was...let's say he wasn't kind...but he worked hard.

> Because I know the rule about ellipses,
> I use them properly.

Using the Ellipsis and Brackets

*

THINK OF BRACKETS [ ] AS CLARIFIERS. You use them in two ways. First, you substitute words and put them within the brackets to make clear to readers what you mean and that you modified the original statement.

"Then [Jesus] told them a story: 'A rich man had a fertile farm that produced fine crops...' "[12] The translation reads, "Then he told..."

Second, you point out a linguistic irregularity, spelling error, or grammatical mistake you want to correct when you quote. When you change a quotation, you follow the irregularity with the Latin *sic* in brackets to indicate the questionable words. *Sic* means "intentionally so written," and grammarians have used it for more than 150 years.

- "None of the students [*sic*] in my class complained," the teacher wrote to the school board. Her original sentence began: None of the twenty-seven, multi-cultural children and seven teens in my class...

- "I don't want anything [*sic*] except justice," the old man wrote in pencil on lined paper. He wrote, "I don't want nothing," and the brackets corrected his grammar.

I use brackets to clarify meanings.
They are not substitutes for parentheses.

---

[12] Luke 12:16.

Who and Whom

*

I SEE THIS MISTAKE APPEAR CONSTANTLY IN PRINT. No one writes *whom* incorrectly—at least not that I've noticed. This will probably die within the next generation, but the rule is still that *whom* is the objective case and the object of a preposition.

Too difficult to remember or too complicated? Try this simple test. Restate the sentence and if you can substitute *him* for *whom* and it makes sense, *whom* is the right word.

- Whom do you wish to see? (I wish to see him. You wouldn't say, I wish to see he.)
- Who will go to the store with me? (You wouldn't say, Him will go to the store with me.)
- Whom can we turn to when we face a financial loss? I would write the sentence: To whom can we turn...even though it may sound stiff to some. (We can turn to him, so *whom* is correct.)

> If I can use *him* instead of *whom*,
> I've used whom correctly.

Rules That Aren't Rules

*

MOST OF US HAVE SEEN those humorous and cleverly reversed rules of grammar that float across the Internet: "Don't use no double negatives" is one. Another says, "I've told you a million times never to exaggerate."

In every such list I've read, they insert one rule that is *not* a rule: "A preposition is a word not to end a sentence with."

Although it's *not* a rule of grammar and appears in no reputable textbook, it's still good advice. The reason isn't because it's a preposition but because prepositions are weak. The same *rule* applies to most adverbs. Consider the difference between these two sentences: 1. He knocked over the box; 2. He knocked the box over. Both make sense, but *box* is stronger than *over* for the end of the sentence.

Let's go back to that supposed rule: A preposition is a word not to end a sentence with. What is the most important word in that sentence? Obviously, it's not *with.* The writer, of course, has to make that determination, but I opt for *preposition,* so I would say: Don't end your sentence with a preposition. Or I could write: A preposition is not a good word with which to end a sentence. That places emphasis on *sentence.* If I chose the word *end* for emphasis, I would have to say, somewhat awkwardly: A preposition is not the word to use for the sentence to end.

I don't avoid ending sentences with prepositions because of any rule. I avoid ending sentences with prepositions because I want strong endings for sentences.

> Because I write strong sentences,
> I avoid ending them with weak words
> such as prepositions or adverbs.

No Such Grammatical Rule
or No Such Rule in Grammar

*

SOMETIMES YOU EMPHASIZE A WORD OR PHRASE by putting them at the beginning of a sentence. That's the second power position. Any element in the sentence, other than the subject, becomes emphatic when placed first. You could say Thelma could never forgive lying. As constructed, the crime or sin receives the emphasis. Suppose, however, you wanted to place *never forgive* in the power position. You might write: Lying is something Thelma could never forgive.

Here's an illustration that shows how we choose what we wish to emphasize in a sentence.

1. Cecil Murphey received a million-dollar advance from Penguin Books last week [not last year].

2. From Penguin Books [not from Doubleday], last week Cecil Murphey received a million-dollar advance.

3. Penguin Books paid a million-dollar advance last week to Cecil Murphey [and not to someone else].

4. Last week, Penguin books gave a million-dollar advance to Cecil Murphey. [Because of word order, *last week* receives the emphasis.]

It's subtle. Most readers wouldn't grasp the difference between the four examples. That's all right, because they don't have to understand the techniques. What readers grasp is that some people write better than others. But you will know what you want to emphasize.

Because I'm a serious writer,
I learn where I want to place the emphasis.

Adjectives Modify
Only Nouns and Pronouns

*

YOU PROBABLY LEARNED THAT IN GRADE SCHOOL, but what happens when you have an adjective that modifies another adjective? To get beyond that rule of grammar, we use the hyphen, which makes both words function as a single adjective.

Consider this sentence: He walked along the *wrought-iron fence*. Without the hyphen, it properly reads, He walked along the wrought, iron fence.

In the following examples, I've inserted the hyphen to make the meaning obvious.

- His *oft-spoken words* echoed through my head.
- He held his four-by-six-inch device. All four words modify *device*.
- He whispered a soft-but-fervent prayer. By hyphenating, all three words function as a single adjective to modify prayer.

I make reading easier because
I remember simple punctuation tips.

Comic-book Writing

*

WE ALSO CALL IT SOUND-EFFECTS WRITING. Even though some writers use sound effects, it shows lack of care about the craft. Such sentences say, "It's good enough and I don't need to work hard." It takes more effort (and creativity) to *show,* but it's also better writing.

- *Snap. Crackle. Pop.* (These three words are also clichés.)
- The gun went bang.
- Slap! Her face burned from the imprint of his hand.

Not only does comic-book writing show sloth, but writers assume that everyone understands what *bang* or *slap* means. For readers to connect with the prose, we need to show *bang* and *snap.*

You can express the noise of a fired gun in many ways. Our word choice guides readers to interpret the intended meaning.

Just as bad is that some writers WRITE IN ALL CAPS.

"WHAT DO YOU WANT?" he screamed.

"GET OUT OF MY LIFE!"

I assume this is again the mark of the insecure writer who wants to make certain that readers grasp the emphasis. All caps insults readers by saying, "Because you aren't clever enough to understand, I'll write in big, shouting letters."

Readers are as bright (or brighter) than I am;
I write in clear word pictures
so they can visualize what I mean.

Watch the Use of *Would*

*

THE HELPING VERB *WOULD* REFERS TO USUAL ACTION. Once you make it clear that you refer to action that's frequent or usual, you don't need to use it again. Or if you've already established it as habitual, you don't need it. Put the rest of the material into the simple past tense.

- Josiah regularly did the butt-scoot boogie as we liked to call it. He would push himself into a sitting position. (*Regularly* shows it's his usual form.) Better: He pushed himself...
- Even the mockingbird in our neighborhood knew the sounds of our house. We would hear beeps and alarms. (The writer had already established that as a regular occurrence.) We heard...I would avoid "we heard" to start a sentence: Beeps and alarms...
- *I'd* get up in the morning like every other mother and take my son to school and I'd go to the tennis courts at the nearby park. After three sets of doubles, I'd hop in the car and I'd head to Macys. (*I'd* means *I would* and the writer established customary behavior with the first word. In the final clause, it should read, I went...I hopped...I headed.)

Would as a helping verb establishes usual behavior.
I need to use it only once.

Outside the Punctuation

*

THE BRITISH DO IT DIFFERENTLY, but Americans punctuate the following sentences this way. That is, we put quotation marks *after* commas, periods, and question marks.

- "I need to go now."
- "Do it then, if that's the way you feel," she said.
- "Why would I want that book?" Mary asked.

However, there is one exception. You place a question mark or exclamation point after the final quotation mark if the quoted material isn't part of the question or exclamation.

- Do you realize there is no Bible verse that reads, "God helps those who help themselves"?

I will remember that punctuation goes inside the quotation marks.

Nouns in Apposition

*

AN APPOSITIVE IS USUALLY A NOUN that *renames* another noun. If you remember that single word, *renames,* you'll have no trouble with this rule.

My friend, Charlie, will go. As written, it means you have only one friend and his name is Charlie. If you have at least one other friend, you omit the commas so that it reads: My friend Charlie will go.

- My wife Shirley likes to read. As written, the sentence means I'm a polygamist. Because I have only one wife, I would write: My wife, Shirley, likes to read. Wife and Shirley refer to the same person.

- His sister Ashleigh's room was painted green. (This means he has more than one sister.)

- We'll visit our close friends Willie and Cissy. (This means you have several close friends.)

Here's an easy way to remember. If you can delete the name and the sentence is still a true statement, you know it's correct: My wife, Shirley, used to be an editor. My wife used to be an editor; Shirley used to be an editor.

If the two words refer to the same person or thing,
I separate them with a comma.

Disembodied Eyes

*

EVEN THOUGH THIS IS WIDELY USED, think how absurd these sentences sound:
- His clear amber eyes soberly sought out and met her blue ones. (Their eyes didn't move out of their bodies.)
- His eyes traveled down to his shoes.
- His eyes returned to the altar while his ears listened to the words.

Readers will understand your meaning, but if you take the words literally, the sentences are ludicrous.

Rather than taking the eyes out of the body, I use words such as *stare, gaze, watch, look,* or *gawk.*

Using *Only*

*

- I only want to eat breakfast. (That person is easy to satisfy and has no other desires in life except breakfast.)
- He only wanted to see Mable. (The writer probably meant he wanted to see only Mable—and not all the others.)
- I only wanted to mail a letter. (I wanted to mail only a letter, not three packages.)

Readers will understand what you mean, but why should they have to figure it out? If you want to write with excellence, you'll use *only* correctly.

Only is a restrictive word;
I use it properly.

Using *More Than*

*

THE PRINCIPLE IS SIMPLE: Use *more than* when you cite items you can count. I also admit this may be another principle serious writers may have to surrender. I choose to make my writing as clear and as grammatically accurate as possible, so I hold to the old rule. I frequently see such constructions in print:

- for over a year;
- had been over six months of questions;
- a colleague of mine for over thirteen years;
- my friend of over thirty years.

I would write *more than* in each of the illustrations above. Use *over* when you *don't* write a specific number:

Over a century ago...

Over a period of years...

I use *more than* with an exact number;
I use *over* when the number is inexact.

Less and Fewer

*

LESS AND FEWER CONVEY THE SAME MEANING—they're the opposite of *more.* You use them differently, just as you distinguish between *more than* and *over.*

Use *fewer* when you count exact numbers; use *less* when you speak generally or use mass nouns.

- I have five fewer pencils than Bert. (I can count the pencils.)
- Wanda has less body mass than I do. (This is a mass noun; it's an inexact number.)

This principle is difficult, so here's my tip: Think of less when you describe distance, money, and time.

At our supermarket store, I used to see the incorrect sign: *15 items or less.* Our store has removed that sign (probably because curmudgeons like me complained). It should read: *15 items or fewer.*

If that sounds strange, it's probably because you've read and heard it that way too often.

As a careful writer,
I use fewer when I can count the number.

And with Numbers

*

I EARNED THREE HUNDRED AND SEVENTY-FIVE DOLLARS. Properly that means $300.75. Or I could write, I earned three hundred seventy-five dollars. Or I'd leave out the decimal or make it a general number such as "I earned about 400 dollars."

Although not quite the same, when some people refer to time past, they'll say, "In the year 19 and 47" or "the year 18 and 65." For years, I thought it was a Southern expression until I heard Scott Pelley use it twice on the evening news.

> When I use numbers,
> I remember that *and* means a decimal point.

That Semicolon

*

THE SEMICOLON IS ALL BUT GONE FROM MODERN WRITING. I like it because the semicolon and I have worked together since eighth grade. Today we tend to write shorter sentences and don't need the semicolon. *However, if you insert the semicolon, use it properly.* Some call it the supercomma. It has two uses.

1.*After a colon and a list.* Example: He owns stock in several places: Paris, Texas; London, Ontario; and Berlin, Wisconsin. Without semicolons readers won't know if you mean three locations or six.

2.The semicolon functions like a soft period to join two closely connected sentences. Both parts must have a subject and a predicate. Example: I like your floppy, silly hat; I don't like your high-heeled shoes. I could have inserted *but* after hat. I could have separated both statements with a period. All three methods are correct.

I often write maxims or aphorisms and use the semicolon because the two statements are closely bound to each other: *I am passionately involved in the process; I am emotionally detached from the result.* A period or a comma would work and most readers aren't aware of the difference. But I'm aware; therefore, I use the semicolon. (Did you notice the punctuation in the previous sentence?)

Here are a few violations. It usually happens because writers don't know the rule and use it to impress.

• Many times he'd imagined this day; thought about how it would go. (There is no subject in the second clause. Use a conjunction and a comma.)

• Guiding at the helm as we crossed a stretch of the Atlantic Ocean, watching flying fish buzz above the waves, snorkeling with giant sea turtles; and an endless variety of fish and coral. (Why a semicolon? The sentence contains 34 words; for modern readers, that's too many. I'd suggest making two sentences and no semicolon.)

• Give us the freedom to choose; life with liberty or life without liberty. (Again, it's incorrect because the second clause isn't a complete sentence. I'd use a colon after choose.)

Unless I'm positive I know how and when to use the semicolon, I won't.

Reflecting Myself

*

MYSELF IS WHAT YOU CALL A REFLECTIVE PRONOUN. That means reflects or repeats a previous pronoun in a different form. That is, you must identify *I* before you use *myself.*

- January 1 was a time of surrender, seeking help from a source far greater than myself. (Far greater than I. It's not *me* or *myself* because the phrase means "far greater than I am great.")
- She gave the money to Maggie and myself. (Incorrect. You have not identified *myself.*)
- I like you better than I like myself. (This is correct because myself reflects or refers to the already-mentioned "I.")

I don't write *myself,*
unless I have already identified who I am.

Sentence Fragments

*

A SENTENCE MUST HAVE A SUBJECT AND A VERB and be able to stand alone as a complete thought. *After I waited for Tom* contains a subject and a verb, but it's not a complete thought.

You probably learned that in school. In informal (that is, commercial) writing, we violate the rule by writing less than whole sentences, but we do it carefully and consciously.

The careful use of fragments can add meaning and power to your writing. For example: I was absolutely happy. For now. The last two words are a fragment, but they raise a question or produce doubt. The fragment is also closely connected to the full sentence it follows.

In the following paragraph, notice the fragments, and yet they make sense:

> They missed the people from whom they had fled. They missed the sight and sound of Africans. Even the smell of their homes. The sing-song chanting of workers in the fields. The tangy smell of wood smoke in the early evening.

Fragments work well (when used cautiously) in action scenes.
In what follows, Jason is running his first marathon:

> He ran past the first group, and was only a dozen yards behind the two leaders. He pushed forward. Too fast. He had to control his pace to win the race. Easy. Easy now. Sneak up behind them.

I used fragments. The first is *Too fast.* I could have written: It was too fast or he moved too quickly. But the purpose is to make readers feel as if they're running with Jason and are inside or beside him. The same for *Easy. Easy now. Sneak up behind them.*

It's all right for me to use sentence fragments occasionally— as long as the meaning is clear.

128

Chronological Order

*

WHEN YOU REFER TO A SERIES OF EVENTS, write them according to the time they occurred, beginning with the earliest.

- Bette Davis won the Oscar in 1938 for her role in *Jezebel* and in 1935 for her performance in *Dangerous.* Common sense says to start with 1935.
- He snacked at 3:00 in the afternoon, 9:00 in the morning, midnight, and at odd hours before dawn. Start with 9:00, which is the earliest.
- He stared at his childhood pictures, showing him when he was a year old, nine months old, sixteen, and seven. The way to correct this one is probably obvious.

When I list time events,
I put them in chronological order
and I begin with the earliest date.

Smaller to the Greater

*

WHEN WRITING A SERIES, go from what's least important and move on to the most. You do this to build the significance of the statements.

- For the next hour, Merlin paced the room, screamed with impatience, and shifted his weight from one foot to the other. The order is ridiculous, so start with the lesser action, which is shifting his weight, and you end with a scream.
- He disliked peppers, loathed celery, and tolerated peas. If you think of the emotional level, tolerated seems the most benign, followed by disliked.

When I write a series of actions,
I begin with the least and move to the greatest.

That and Which

*

Over the years, a number of rules have risen and died. One rule governs *which* and *that*, although most people don't know or ignore it.

Use *that* to begin a restrictive clause; use *which* for everything else.

So what's a restrictive clause? It's the part of a sentence we can't delete and still convey the meaning we want.

1. Emails that carry a brief subject line get read more often.

The clause *that carry a brief subject line* is restrictive. If you deleted it, the sentence would read: Emails get read more often—and you've distorted the information. The difference seems obvious. The word *that* limits or confines (restricts) the type of emails to which we refer.

2.Loud voices, which we hear constantly, annoy us. If you remove *which we hear constantly,* the meaning of the sentence doesn't suffer.

If I can't delete the clause without changing the meaning, I use *that*.

Who and That

*

IN EIGHTH-GRADE ENGLISH, you probably learned a simple rule: If you refer to people or animals, use who; if you refer to objects, use *that*. Most people tend to use *that* constantly and rarely infuse a sentence with a *who*.

Today the distinction has largely vanished. This is one of those rules that many people don't know or don't care about. My wife, who is my proofreader, cares deeply about this distinction. (Did you notice the use of *who?*)

> *Who* refers to people or animals; otherwise I use *that*.

Who and Whose

*

TO COMPLICATE THIS ISSUE, use *whose* with people or objects because it's the plural possessive of *who. However,* English has no plural possessive for *that.*

1. Those students whose work is incomplete will fail the course.

2. Those streetlights whose rays shine into my bedroom prevent my sleeping soundly.

> I use *whose* as the plural possessive
> of people and objects.

Watch Your Nors

*

I READ THESE TWO SENTENCES RECENTLY and both are incorrect.

1. Hilda didn't want his money nor his property.
2. Neither John or Ralph planned to attend Samantha's wedding.

Think of *neither* and *nor* as a couple and especially as nor being dependent on neither. They don't like being separated. (And both words start with the letter *n*, to remind you.) If you invite neither into your sentence, you want to include nor. And nor refuses to stand alone.

Neither and *nor* are two words that like to appear together.

P.S. Sometimes you use *neither* and imply *nor*. If you're talking to Ken and Ralph, you say, "Neither of you may go." You imply neither Ken nor Ralph.

Oral or Verbal?

*

THIS IS ONE OF THOSE DISTINCTIONS I have to think through when I'm writing. The use of *oral* doesn't seem to trouble anyone—that means words you speak. The problem comes with *verbal*, because it's not limited to spoken words. The words can be written or spoken.

"I have a verbal agreement," Mac said.

"Was it written or oral?" Tina asked.

Tina's question is correct. *Verbal* refers to the use of words, not to the form of communication. Verbal communication can be written or spoken.

If I refer to words spoken aloud, I use *oral;* if I refer to the use of words, written or oral, I use *verbal.*

ATM or HIV?

*

KAREN WITHDREW MONEY from the ATM machine at the drugstore.

"I think that man has the HIV virus," Ellie said.

Although I hear both sentences, they contain redundancy or what a friend calls an echo. If you like saying something twice, don't change anything. ATM means *Automated Teller Machine*. HIV is an acronym for *human immunodeficiency virus*. The final letter of both words explains what they are so why repeat?

> When I use acronyms such as HIV or ATM,
> I don't repeat the last letter as a word.

Did You *Lose* the Knot
or Did You *Loose* It?

*

IT DEPENDS. If you lose a knot, it means you've misplaced it or you can't find it. If you loose a knot, you untie it. Many people pronounce both words the same, which is confusing. (Pronounce *lose* with a z sound at the end.)

Think of loose as the opposite of *tight;* lose refers to something you no longer have.

> If I lose it, I don't have it;
> if I loose it, I free it from restraint.

Is it Valuable or Invaluable?

*

THE WORDS ARE FAIRLY CLOSE IN MEANING, but here's how I keep them straight. If something is valuable, it's costly or worth a great deal, and we generally put a dollar figure with it. If it's invaluable, it means it's so important that I can't put a price on it.

1. Sue's engagement ring was valuable because it cost Ned $25,000.

2. Your expertise is invaluable—I could never have figured out how to set up my computer without your assistance.

In the second example, unless your friend charges you, the help is so deeply appreciated you can't put a money figure on what it's worth.

If it's valuable, I can put a price on it;
if there is no way to calculate the worth, it's invaluable.

Started to and Began to

*

WATCH THE USE OF THOSE EXPRESSIONS because they imply incomplete action or action that's interrupted. I began to eat my cereal but the phone rang. I started to watch TV but fell asleep.

Too many writers throw in such expressions, unaware that they refer to *unfinished action.*

In the examples below, the writing is not only more accurate but stronger if you omit those expressions.

- Jana began to move around the area. (Jana moved…)
- I have begun to include singing or listening to inspirational music (I include singing…)
- The poetry of Edgar Allan Poe began to take on new meaning. (The poetry of Edgar Allan Poe took…)

Unless I mean interrupted activity,
I avoid using *started to* and *began to.*

Shooting Glances

*

GIVING SHRUGS AND SHOOTING GLANCES are not only odd statements but also weak writing. I've read these words with increasing frequency in novels. One writer uses a quirky phrase, another author copies it, and still others pick up the expression. Good writing carries a natural tone and if you make readers blink with an odd phrase, instead of admiring your creativity, they're apt to stop reading.

- *She gave a gasp of pain* is weaker than *She gasped in pain.*
- Jean gave a small, impatient jerk of her head. (Just let her jerk her head.)
- She shot him a smile and walked on. (I don't understand what that means. To shoot doesn't sound friendly or kind and the context doesn't provide a clue.)
- She impaled him with a glance. (That makes no sense. A glance is quick, something that takes place so quickly we don't get details. Can a glance thrust a spear through another?)

I don't use weak verbs to replace stronger ones.
I don't use odd statements that cause readers to blink.

140

Adverb Endings

*

THE COMMON PRACTICE OF CHANGING ADJECTIVES TO ADVERBS by adding the -ly has changed. In English grammar, we classify words by their function and not by their spelling. *Smile* can be a noun or a verb as it is in this odd sentence: She smiled at his smile. *Smile* is a verb (action) and a noun.

Until recent years, we wrote *firstly* but modern, informal usage settles for *first*. First, he finished his task and then he ate. (Tells us when he ate.) Scholarly writing still holds to the adding of the –ly.

For the rest of us, *importantly* has become *important*. Most important, he did his job well. If we don't delete the ending, the writing sounds stilted or pompous.

▪ First, I want your attention, and second, I want you to smile when I pause. In the past we would have written firstly and secondly.

▪ Most important, listen to your mother.

▪ The highway sign read, "Drive slow." *Slow* is an adjective and *slowly* is an adverb, but modern usage has changed the rule.

> I remind myself that modern usage tends to strip the -ly from adverbs.

I Think, I Know

*

AVOID USING EXPRESSIONS such as I *believe, I think, I know,* or *it seems to me.* To use them weakens the statement. People read your words in print and that makes you an authority. If you say what you believe or think without equivocating, your words carry authority.

- I believe that telling the truth is the honorable way to live. (Telling the truth is the honorable way to live. Can you hear the difference?)
- I think my methods bring results. (Maybe my methods do; I'm not sure.)
- I know that there will be a day of reckoning for all people.
- It seems to me that our neighborhood is deteriorating.

When I avoid expressions such as *I think,* my writing is stronger and carries more impact.

This and That

*

In recent years, writers have tended to use *this* in relating an account when they should have written *that.*

- Use *this* when you refer to the present or something physically near;
- Use *that* when you refer to the past or something far away.

Here are examples of the misuse of *this.*

- Write a brief summary of the ways you could show this person's selfless love. (Unless the person is physically present, use *that.*)
- Nothing in our conversation prepared me for this question. (The context was past tense, as shown by *prepared*, so someone asked the question in the past.)
- On this particular day my intuition kept tugging at me to turn the car around. (*That* is probably better. If the author uses *this* to make it what we call present continuous tense, the sentence should read: On this particular day my intuition *keeps* tugging at me... Or she could have shifted it to the past tense: On that particular day, my intuition continued to...)

In each of these three examples, *that* is probably the better word choice.

Because I am a growing writer, I'm careful to distinguish between *this* and *that.*

143

Contractions

*

USE CONTRACTIONS; otherwise, the writing sounds stilted. Write the way people talk.

- "Could you not have spared me this disgrace?"
- He was not surprised. It was not my first arrest.
- The sailors on that ship did not believe in the God of the Jews.

If you're writing an academic paper, you probably won't use contractions. If you write dialog and want to show a formal, stuffy individual, don't use contractions. For all other writing, however, you communicate better by writing the way most of us talk—with contractions. A writer of historical fiction researched and said contractions first appeared in print around 1811. That's 200 years to get used to simplified language.

I write for the general public
so I keep my language informal.

6

* * *

Improve Your Fiction

Purple-prose Writing

*

FOR SIX YEARS, I TAUGHT MY OWN MENTORING CLINICS. I varied their length but at first they lasted from three days and finally down to one full day, so I could work individually with writers. I found the same problems occurring in many manuscripts. Eventually I developed a list of common problems—weaknesses that I saw repeatedly.

As I deal with them in this series, some will include items I've mentioned in previous chapters. I sent out a handful of common problems before the clinics on six occasions, but it was as if they hadn't read them. They didn't seem to grasp some of the principles until they saw the weaknesses in their own writings.

Purple-prose writing is a long-used term that refers to extravagant overwriting. The term usually refers to descriptions that call attention to themselves. I see this in the writings of insecure writers who are afraid to use simple state-of-being verbs like *is, are,* and *were.* To avoid simple words and the passive voice they try to paint pictures with excessive expressions.

The writers want to sound powerful and dramatic, but the sentences become melodramatic and over-the-top prose. Here are a few examples:

- He struggled to tame the pounding wave of thoughts that threatened to blur his focus.
- His throat tightened as fear swept over his brother's face like the shadow they chased across the field behind their house when an airplane flew over.
- The light of day kept my loneliness in the shadows of my mind, but as soon as the lights were out, my thoughts went to that despair.
- The air kept the stillness captive as men held their breath in anticipation.
- Rapidly firing her digital camera, she captured the dress rehearsal fever staining the cheeks of several antsy actors.
- Lib placed a hand over the traitorous butterflies coasting in her belly.
- Rand stood, mouth agape. He snapped his mouth shut. Jaw and neck muscles bulged as he stormed out.

My best writing is the most easily understood, because the meaning is obvious and the words are simple.

146

Purple-prose Punctuation

*

THIS SHOWS UP IN TWO WAYS. First is the pause (...) which means slow, deliberate thinking. Purple-prose punctuation occurs when writers:
- don't trust their writing;
- don't trust readers to interpret;
- make an attempt to be dramatic—and fail;
- write the words as they hear them inside their heads, including the pauses between the phrases.

The pause is properly called an ellipsis (...). When used as an obvious pause, it's effective. "I was thinking...maybe..."

Too many writers try to use the device as a dramatic pause to heighten the emotional impact. *It rarely works.* Trust your readers to get the point without going melodramatic.

- She hopes against all hope that Ben isn't dead...that he'll soon return...that she'll finally be able to tell him the truth...
- Scenes of my own arrest flashed rapidly...my disgrace...my loss of innocence....

If I write clearly,
readers will grasp my meaning.

Purple-prose Punctuation

*

THE SECOND PURPLE-PROSE PUNCTUATION PROBLEM is the exclamation mark. If you consider the exclamation mark noisy and loud, you'll rarely use it. I often tell students, "The most obvious mark of insecure writers is the use of the exclamation mark. They shout several times on every page because they don't trust their ability to communicate effectively." (And yes, in my early writing days, I seasoned my manuscripts with exclamation marks.) Here are a few examples from my students.

- It came from below them!
- Jean shivered!
- Of course he would not give it back!
- How luxurious the life of a bride would be!

> I don't use the exclamation mark—
> unless nothing else works.

Setting and Background in Fiction

*

BACKGROUND IS IMPORTANT, ESPECIALLY IN FICTION. It gives the sense of readers being there. But you need to be careful and do it well.

My friend Julie Garmon, who writes for *Guideposts,* said the editors hate stories that begin with a weather report. I'd go so far as to say that most readers don't want a weather report anywhere in the article or book unless it pertains to what's happening.

Yet you do need background—but it works best when you slip in a sentence or two at a time instead of lengthy passages that trace the sun from its rising to midday.

Here's lesson number one: Make your setting and background unobtrusive. Ask yourself this question: If I leave out this sentence or this paragraph, will readers miss it? Will it detract from what I want to say? Background is exactly what the word means. Too many writers make it the foreground.

I make settings and backgrounds props to enhance my fiction. They don't call attention to themselves.

Setting and Background in Fiction

*

DON'T FAKE THE BACKGROUND. Don't guess. Look up details, even if they seem insignificant. I read a novel in which a man took a direct flight from San Francisco to Minneapolis. One of my friends informed him, "You can't get a direct flight."

Minor detail? Perhaps, but there are always readers who know.

By contrast, an editor wrote my agent, "I've never been to Africa, but Murphey makes the setting real." (He didn't offer a contract, but I appreciated his comment.)

I read a bio in which a man, in 1934, chewed Bazooka Bubble Gum. The bazooka was a World War II weapon and the gum came out of that era. The author meant Fleers Double Bubble gum. It was a minor detail, but it caused me to distrust the writer's integrity on important facts.

If readers can't trust you on minor details, how can they know you're correct on important things?

I strive for accuracy with details
because I want to win the trust of readers.

Setting and Background in Fiction

*

"I HAD PLANNED TO SET THE NOVEL IN VENICE because I've been there," she said, "but it seems that every fifth novelist sets stories in that city."

To which I answered, "So what?"

Just because hundreds of others have used New York City or Paris doesn't mean you can't feature those locations.

Make certain you get the facts straight. Beyond that, you add your special perceptions.

If I wrote about Paris, I'd certainly mention the beautifully planted rows of plane trees (what we Americans call sycamores) and I'd certainly want to include Chartres Cathedral. My particular insight would make the location "mine" because of my voice and style.

If you make your story take place in a famous place such as Zurich or Athens, be accurate. You also want to insert a few details that most readers won't know.

For instance, you might have the hero racing down Station Road in London, trying to elude his abductors. He rushes into the Betford Betting Shop. (I looked up the name and location on the Web.)

One or two sentences will give readers not only a sense of place, but many of them haven't heard of a betting shop. That adds to your story.

> When I insert little-known information,
> I add value to my story.

Setting and Background in Fiction

*

ON AMAZON.COM, I READ A REVIEW of a famous literary novel that said the author must have been reading a roadmap when he wrote one particular chapter. For twenty pages the author details the places he stops to eat breakfast, have morning coffee, and so on. None of it, apparently, was germane to the plot. (I checked out the book at the library and I agreed with the reviewer.)

Some writers become enamored with travel information and seem to think it's important to everyone.

Here's the question you need to ask: Will readers care? Does the travel information add suspense or depth to your story?

A writer friend said, "I don't give any background unless it has some direct bearing on the story. Otherwise readers might ask, 'Why did she put that in the book?'"

I won't clog my prose with long passages about background or travel.

Setting and Background in Fiction

*

WHEN DONE WELL, BACKGROUND INFORMATION DOESN'T INTRUDE. Unskilled writers feel they have to give a litany of details to show their scenes are authentic. We make scenes believable by a sentence or two at a time.

Years ago I wrote a novel set in Kenya in 1950, and the major characters drive from Nairobi toward Lake Victoria. The heroine avoids talking to the hero and stares out the window. I inserted one sentence to enable readers to sense the authentic setting: "Kikuyu women toiled up steep, red paths, bending forward under the heavy loads of firewood strapped onto their backs."

That's all. A few pages later, I slipped in a one-sentence description of a tea plantation, which she pointed out to him to cut off personal conversation.

If you insert the few-but-significant details, you show readers you know what you're writing about and that your words are authentic.

I don't stop the action to provide background. The setting becomes a minor character of the story.

Setting and Background in Fiction

*

IF YOU CHOOSE THE RIGHT BACKGROUND, the setting itself can become an element of suspense.

What if she is to meet someone at the Vietnam Memorial in Washington, DC, after dark?

What about being the only person waiting for a MARTA train in Atlanta and a man comes down the escalator? He stares at her. With his right hand in his coat pocket, he steps toward her.

What if you take a shortcut during a snowstorm and your car breaks down in an area with no houses around?

> The background I choose
> can add suspense.

Setting and Background in Fiction

*

DON'T BE AFRAID TO USE ORDINARY SETTINGS. What's wrong with a family farm near Anadarko, Oklahoma? The city square in Marietta, Georgia? You drive across the Verrazano Bridge toward Brooklyn and you realize you don't have money for the toll? What if you see your worst enemy across the aisle in a Macy's?

By setting your book in non-exotic places, you write about the kind of people and occupations readers easily understand. You submerge readers into reality so you can take them into suspenseful happenings.

When I have ordinary people doing ordinary things I provide a sense of reality and prepare them to accept the extraordinary turn of the story.

Setting and Background in Fiction

*

DON'T UNDERESTIMATE THE IMPORTANCE OF PLACE AND TIME. I call them the grounding factors. Two questions you don't want readers to ask are: 1). Where is this taking place? 2). What's the time period?

Suppose you have a story in which a young woman wants to make a favorable impression on a sailor on leave whom she invited for dinner. She picks tomatoes and carrots from her victory garden before she stares at her ration book to see if she has enough points for a roast.

I haven't specifically given you time or place, but you've probably sensed this is World War II (victory garden and ration book). The other implication is that it's in a city or a town.

> Good writing *implies* more about setting
> than it says in words.

What Does Dialog Do?

*

THE ANSWER IS: MANY THINGS.

In real life, people speak in general, long-winded diatribes, or mention twenty things before they focus on what they want to say. In print, we need to delete the clutter and get to the point.

If a person is loquacious, we can insert a statement or two in the middle of the lecture and readers understand.

Here's an example: James paused and gulped the last of his Coke, hardly aware that Amos had zoned out and Aimee had mentally planned her dinner menu for a full week.

Make your characters speak less than people actually do (even in nonfiction), and speak more the way real people wish they spoke.

In each of the pages that follow, I'll emphasize one aspect of dialog, even though I am conveying several different purposes.

Conversation thrusts you into a scene, which is true in nonfiction and fiction. Your readers become characters in the ongoing narrative. They feel the tension and the conflict. They "hear" the dialog along with the character.

Good dialog isn't realistic, although it needs to sound like people talking. But it's more. Although it seems obvious, good dialog has a purpose and skilled writers make it accomplish more than one thing at a time.

"Don't tell me how to do my job." James stared at his boss. "You have enough problems with your own work."

"Yeah? Then why am I the boss and you work for me?"

"I don't work *for* you. I work under you—like a serf."

We're in the scene and most of us have felt like James at some time in our lives. Dialog makes us identify with or feel the words of at least one character.

When I write dialog well,
I involve readers so they feel they become part of the scene.

What Does Dialog Do?

*

GOOD DIALOG ADVANCES THE NARRATIVE. Dialog furthers the action and intensifies the story.

> On the second ring, Phoebe answered her cell. "I can't talk to you right now, Joan. I'm in my car, and I'm on the way to Gerald's funeral."
> "I can't believe you'd go—not after all he did—"
> "I can't drive and talk at the same time." Phoebe closed the phone and mumbled. "She means *she* wouldn't go to the funeral."

In the brief dialog, I advanced the plot. Phoebe is going to the funeral and Joan is against it. (Tension builds.) Readers will realize Gerald did something terrible (perhaps many things). She is going anyway, which implies she has forgiven him or perhaps it wasn't something he did to her but to Joan. (This builds suspense.) Phoebe brushes off Joan. (This calls attention to the relationship of the two women.) From the final sentence, we realize the issue is Joan's and not Phoebe's.

My dialog needs a purpose.
Readers may not be aware of where it's going, but I know.

What Does Dialog Do?

*

DIALOG DEVELOPS OR SHOWS READERS SOMETHING ABOUT YOUR CHARACTERS. You can also use conversation to reveal attitudes and motivation.

Your characters make it clear that they act or respond for good reason. Dialog can effectively expose those reasons. If you do it well, readers absorb the information without your having to explain what you're doing.

How about this: "My dear, I would be the last person—absolutely the last person in town to say this—but I felt you ought to know. I mean, after all, everyone is talking about it."

What does the above-sentence tell you about the speaker? Rather than your telling readers, they probably get the negative feeling toward the speaker.

What does the following say about your character? "Hate you? How could I?" She touched his cheek and said, "No matter what you've done, didn't you realize that I would forgive you?"

My dialog implies something about the speaker as well as conveys information to readers.

159

What Does Dialog Do?

*

DIALOG DEMONSTRATES THE EMOTIONAL STATE OR ATTITUDE OF THE SPEAKER. In the illustration below, Herbert announces at a family gathering that he has received a million-dollar advance on his first novel.

"That's exciting and wonderful! You deserve every cent."

"It's quite pleasant to hear of your achievements. Thank you for telling us."

"Yes, it is good news but think of all the tax you'll have to pay."

"You are such a simple optimist, aren't you? They'll find a way to trick you."

Four speakers and yet in the brief comments, readers already know something about each character.

If I write dialog well,
readers will know the actors' attitudes by their words.

160

What Does Dialog Do?

*

DIALOG CONVEYS NEEDED INFORMATION SUCCINCTLY.

"I want to drive to the State Fair by myself." He held up his new driver's license.

Brad's father shook his head. "It's a trip of more than five hours and most of the roads were damaged by the flood."

The information is probably quite obvious—the State Fair, the length of time it takes, and the bad roads. We also have a hint of tension between the father and son. The new license tells us something about Brad's lack of experience.

As part of the dialog,
my characters convey needed information.

What Does Dialog Do?

*

GOOD DIALOG BUILDS SUSPENSE AND INTENSIFIES THE PLOT.

"What did you and Rory talk about?" Helen asked.

"I'm too distraught to talk about it." Elaine twisted her handkerchief and refused to look at her sister.

"Forget distraught. What did he say? Does he want to marry you or not?"

"Yes..."

"But what? Did he say anything about me?"

In those few lines, your readers see a woman grilling her sister. The final question, "Did he say anything about me?" sounds odd. The question is about marrying Elaine, so why does Helen bring herself into the situation? Why is Elaine disturbed?

My dialog moves the story forward
by intensifying the drama
and hinting at things readers don't yet know.

What Does Dialog Do?

*

DIALOG CONTROLS THE PACE. If the story is moving too slowly, your dialog can speed it up.

The couple has driven for hours without stopping for food. Erica hasn't eaten anything since the night before and she's hungry. Bruce wants to keep driving.

"I'm hungry."

"You won't starve."

"There! See there's a Cracker Barrel ahead—"

"Someone might recognize me—"

"You think the whole world is on alert for you?"

"Don't want to take chances."

"No one pays much attention to anyone these days. Please, can't—"

"Not yet."

I pick up the pace by using short sentences or sentence fragments.

What Does Dialog Do?

*

IF THE PACE IS MOVING TOO QUICKLY, USE DIALOG TO SLOW IT DOWN. Characters can pause, reflect, or stare into space.

"I'm hungry and I want to stop and eat."

Bruce shook his head. "I don't know…I'm not sure it's safe…"

"No one will pay attention to us." She turned toward him, resisting the urge to grab his arm.

Bruce stared out the window. "I'm thinking…I'm thinking."

I can use reflective dialog
to slow the pace.

What Does Dialog Do?

*

DIALOG READS FASTER THAN NARRATIVE. If you sense you're giving too much background, weather, or scenery, let them talk about it.

> "Is it always this hot in West Texas?"
> "Not always. Sometimes the temperature hits about 110 degrees."
> "How much longer do we have to travel on this flat highway?"

The dialog isn't very exciting, but we give readers weather information in the lips of a character.

And here's another rule. If you, the author, call attention to weather conditions, it implies you have a purpose. Perhaps their car will overheat. Maybe they'll run out of gas on the long highway, and the unrelenting heat will make it difficult to get out and walk.

My dialog always has a purpose—and often more than one purpose.

What Does Dialog Do?

*

DIALOG SUMS UP ACTION OF THE PLOT. A character can explain in a few sentences for another person not present to the action.

"Sara can give you all the details in her report, but it comes down to this. DataBay has offered forty a share—"

"That's not as much as it's worth—"

"The board decided to take it anyway." Bart shrugged. "It was a rigged meeting."

In a few sentences of dialog,
I can sum up pages of action.

How Do I Write Good Dialog?

*

DON'T BE AFRAID OF *SAID*. It's invisible and readers don't notice. The same is true for words such as *ask, answer,* or *reply*. If you use stronger verbs, you take the emphasis off *what* and you stress *how* it was spoken.

"I love you," she said.
"I love you," she whispered.
"I love you," she shouted.

Catch the difference? Why did she whisper? Or shout? Immediately readers' thoughts go to the reason for the manner in which the person speaks, and that moves it away from what she says.

> If I use simple words like *said* for dialog attributes, those words become invisible to readers.

How Do I Write Good Dialog?

*

USE INCOMPLETE SENTENCES. Let characters interrupt each other.

> "I do not wish to see you tomorrow or any other day. You have disappointed me too many times. This is over," Robert said.
>
> "But I will change. I know I can change," Emily said and cried, "I am different now. Truly, I am."

Contrast that with this:

> "I do not wish to see you tomorrow or any other day," Robert said.
>
> "But I love you—"
>
> "You've disappointed me too many times and—"
>
> "I know, but I can change." Emily wiped tears from her eyes. "I know I can do—"
>
> "It's too late to—"
>
> "No, please, Robert. Please give me another chance."

In the first example, they both spoke in full sentences without contractions. We got the information, but there was little emotion involved. The second helps us become part of the scene.

> To make dialog more realistic,
> I have characters interrupt each other.

How Do I Write Good Dialog?

*

INDIVIDUALIZE YOUR CHARACTERS. Don't make all of them sound the same. If done well, your readers will know who is talking by the way they speak. Women generally speak differently from men and children from adults.

> "Can I go? Can I go? I'll do my chores later."
>
> "May I go with you? I assure you that I'll be on my best behavior."
>
> "I'd sure like to go with you. I'm handy with tools and I have a strong back."
>
> "I wish very much to go, but I require space for my luggage and my precious baby, Sniffy."
>
> "To go with you would be of great pleasure, dear sir, if you would consider offering me space in your carriage."

The dialog above is a bit extreme, but each person speaks differently and you learn something about who they are by their word choices.

> ## My dialog identifies characters and their speech patterns.

How Do I Write Good Dialog?

*

DON'T SNEAK IN INFORMATION THAT'S NOT RELEVANT TO YOUR NARRATIVE. Although talkative people may sit next to you in an airplane, you bore readers by giving them the backstory of a character.

If you want to give readers backstory, use dialog.

Here's how one student began her story. Two women sit next to each other on a plane. One of them has read a letter and begins to cry softly. The woman in the next seat asks, "Is there something wrong?"

> "I've finished reading a letter for the seventh time from my sister, Marilyn Hamilton, who lives in Moline, Illinois. Her husband, John, died 18 months ago, and she has been quite lonely since then. We had a fight nine years ago this month, and I assumed she was over her grief—or at least she ought to be. She wrote me a letter. It's the first word from her in nine years. Wrote me? Can you imagine that? She could have called me, but she didn't. I'm the forgiving one in the family and I forgave her long ago. So I agreed to come for a visit."

This is too much information packed into a single piece of dialog. The student said it was her way to introduce Marilyn, who would become her central character. If the scene is important to the story, you, as the author, need to use two pages of dialog to bring out the various points.

For example, take the first sentence and start the dialog going.

> "I just finished reading a letter for the seventh time from my sister, Marilyn Hamilton—"
> "Seventh time? You must have it memorized by now."
> "Just about. The words are so hurtful—"
> "So why do you torture yourself by re-reading?"
> "I don't know, but she has a way of saying exactly the things that cause me pain."
> "Put it aside then and—"
> "Oh, she didn't write terrible things in this letter. That's the problem."
> Her seat companion frowned. "I don't under—"

See what the student could have done? Readers also learn a great deal about the woman with the letter even though she's using it as an opportunity to castigate her sister.

When I write backstory, I keep readers interested by helping them see the attitude of the narrator.

Insert Beats into Your Dialog

*

BEATS REFER TO PHYSICAL GESTURES, PAUSES, OR THOUGHTS from the character. Such interruptive phrases or sentences avoid the criticism of "talking heads." You show real time and actions, and the dialog includes more than words.

You don't need many beats, but you probably need a few.

> "I owe you so much. You took me under contract when no one was interested. I'm grateful for that. But I'm going to sign with MullMedia."

Four statements and nothing is emphatic. The final statement can be powerful. To do that, use a beat to emphasize it.

> "I owe you so much. You took me under contract when no one was interested. I'm grateful for that." Troy stared at his feet and added, "But I'm going to sign with MullMedia."

A single beat enables readers to absorb the first three statements and prepares them to "hear" the fourth because of the pause. That's what good beats do.

What he did isn't as important as the action and the mood you want readers to grasp. He could stare, turn, look out the window, knock over a cup, or get up and say his final words as he leaves the room.

By contrast, more than a single beat in a paragraph ruins the effect.

> "I owe you so much," Troy said as he smiled at Marvin. "You took me under contract when no one was interested." He picked up a fork and balanced it on his index finger. "I'm grateful for that." Troy stared at his feet and added, "But I'm going to sign with MullMedia." He threw down the fork and pushed back from the table.

Small, carefully inserted bits of action can bring a scene alive by developing character, furthering the story, and building suspense—the same qualities of good dialog. Beats enable readers to picture what's going on and it also interrupts what could be long passages of dialog.

Remind yourself that beats have a purpose. Be certain what you want to accomplish before you insert a sliver of action.

I use beats to enhance a scene;
I don't allow the action to disrupt the scene.

Insert Beats into Your Dialog

*

"I'M A HARD WORKER and you won't have any complaints about me. I worked from 1933 to 1935 with the CCC." The CCC was the Civilian Conservation Corps. "I promise you, I won't let you down."

Although it's not a physical gesture, it's what we call a telling statement. The non-dialog sentence functions like a beat by injecting information to clarify the meaning for readers.

I sneak in information.
If I do it well, readers won't notice.

Four Viewpoints

*

POINT OF VIEW (POV) refers to what goes on inside the head of one person during a scene or a book. The modern rule has been to stay in one POV. I could also say that you become that person on whom you focus, and readers know how the POV individual sees life. New writers tend to jump from head to head within a scene, and often they're not aware of what they're doing. (That style of writing isn't wrong, but it takes great skill. It's often called omniscient POV.)

During the past few years, however, I've seen the omniscient or universal point of view creeping into the writing of best-selling authors. For instance, I skimmed the first chapter of *Fear Factor* by well-known novelist, Robert Harris.

On page 4, readers are in the head of Alex Hoffman. At the bottom of the page, Harris switches to the wife's POV, and on the following page he ends her POV with this paragraph: "She paused in the doorway and considered him for a moment. He still looked young for forty-two.... She sighed and went upstairs." The next paragraph shifts back to the husband: "Hoffman had known for years that..."[13]

I'll discuss the unlimited third-person point of view. Even though it's valid, it's difficult to pull off and to maintain.

In the example I copied above, a smoother writer would have made a scene cut when the wife went upstairs. It's quite a jump from her going upstairs to what's going on inside his head. I suggest writers stay with a single POV. It's clearer to readers, and it enables the author to focus on one person.

> I decide which POV
> I want to use.

---

[13] *Fear Factor*, Robert Harris (New York: Knopf, 2011), p. 5.

Four Viewpoints

*

LET'S SAY YOU'VE CHOSEN FIRST-PERSON POV. Think of yourself as "I," so you cannot possibly know how another character feels or thinks.

Suppose you're in first person and you look at Jamie. "His angry countenance frightened me." How do you know he's angry? You can assume such an attitude, but maybe it's only indigestion or he's thinking of his loss in a bad business deal.

Try it this way: "The look on his face frightened me. Jamie had a right to be angry...."

If you want to vary points of view, the easy way is to remain in one POV for an entire scene. Give us a break to show a scene change and move into another POV.

Here's one way to do it. Olivia and Peter argue over whether it's time to consider having a baby. We're in Olivia's head and she explains why she's not ready to have children.

> "I still want to enjoy my life—do things I can't do after the children come. My mother was tied down from age nineteen until she was nearly forty. She gave up too much."
>
> "I've heard your words before, but I know differently." Peter stared into her dark eyes and said in his coldest voice, "You don't want to give up your six-figure-a-year job..."

Once I decide on one point of view
I stay with it for the entire scene.

Four Viewpoints

*

POINT OF VIEW IS THE PERSPECTIVE FROM WHICH YOU TELL A STORY or anecdote and it applies to fiction and nonfiction. Some say it's the single, most important choice you have to make. I wouldn't go that far, but POV influences how readers perceive the story.

POV answers:

- Who is my main character?
- Which character do I want readers to empathize with or understand?
- How do I want readers to view the setting?

If you chose your POV well, your writing flows. One expert said, "POV is the glue that holds the story together. It also dictates what kind of description we use and which characters get to do the describing."

Suppose the Old Testament story of Joseph and his brothers was written in the POV of Gad? Could he have seen the wickedness of his own heart? (See Genesis chapters 37 to 50.) Probably not.

I use different perspectives
to bring out distinctive aspects of a story.

Four Viewpoints

*

POINT OF VIEW (POV) CAN BE DIFFICULT TO GRASP; it often takes writers a long time to understand. I'll explain each of the four points of view.

First person means you write the story from the "I" viewpoint. When constructed well, this brings about a personal connection with the narrator. Many detective and private eye novels thrust the narrator into the middle of the action. Readers can identify with and become the "I" who solves the problem.

Gothic novels are no longer popular, but they focused on the first person's perception. Gothics began with *Jane Eyre* and include *Rebecca* as an outstanding modern version. The "I" narrator is an insecure, sensitive heroine in a castle or mansion, often isolated, and her life is frequently threatened.

The power of first-person accounts is that they foreshadow events, often evil or catastrophic, through the foreboding or troubled heart of the protagonist.

In the older gothics, they often used the *If-only-I-had-known* technique to create suspense. Readers experienced doubt, fear, and insecurity along with the narrator. Because readers *are* the narrator, they learn only when the narrator does and that can create suspense.

> First-person POV works for specific reasons.
> Before I try it, I'll be sure it works for me.

Four Viewpoints

*

"BEGINNERS LOVE USING FIRST PERSON," an agent said many years ago. She pointed out that, when written well, the writing gives an immediacy to the story.

When I ghostwrite an autobiography, first-person POV is the only option I consider and for that very reason. *Gifted Hands* that I wrote for Dr. Ben Carson begins like this:

"And your daddy isn't going to live with us anymore."

"Why not?" I asked again, choking back the tears...

In *90 Minutes in Heaven*, first person made sense because the entire book revolves around Don Piper and what he experienced.

I've written a total of four books for Don Piper. The other books carry Don's name and mine, which makes me the co-writer. Our editor insisted on staying with the first person and I had no problem with that. Chapter 66, for example, from our second book, *Daily Devotions Inspired by 90 Minutes in Heaven*, begins:

I survived because of prayer.

I survived because one man felt God impress on him to pray for me, even though the EMTs said I was dead. He prayed anyway.

I remind myself that the first-person narrator is an observer and also a character or participant.

Four Viewpoints

*

PEOPLE USED TO ADVISE WRITERS to turn their autobiographies into novels. In my opinion it rarely works, and especially when it's written in first person-POV.

If you attempt to write that way, you create problems because *you*, the story's narrator, aren't the first person. You create a character and see life and events through that person, but you're writing fiction, not nonfiction.

If you try it, the tendency will be to stay close to the facts and thus limit the scope of the book. The book tends to have a kind of wooden tone because you operate only with facts.

As one agent said, "You're too close to the scene of the crime and you have no perspective." She meant that trying to make your experience into fiction tends to take away the spontaneity and imaginative plot twists.

The worst defense you can offer for trying first-person fiction based on reality is, "But it really happened."

So what?

It's not whether it happened, but whether it's believable. As the adage goes, "Truth is stranger than fiction." When you chose fiction, you cut away the lines that kept you tied to literal truth. Your responsibility is to provide a good read—an entertaining, imaginative story.

> My worst defense for a bad novel is,
> "But it really happened."

Four Viewpoints

*

HERE ARE A FEW THINGS YOU NEED TO CONSIDER if you tackle first-person POV.

1. Your readers can know only what your protagonist knows. You can't have any scenes in which the central character is not involved. (A few writers, such as James Patterson, have developed a first-person/third-person style. Alex Cross speaks in first person; the antagonist, in alternating chapters, appears in third-person.)

2. In older works, such as *The Razor's Edge,* W. Somerset Maugham himself acts as narrator and tells the story of Larry Darrell and his spiritual journey. That observer approach has gone out of style. Today, your lead character tells the story. You stay totally inside that head all the way through.

3. One drawback is the awkwardness when the protagonist speaks of himself or herself. In third-person POV, the lead can be objective, but it's difficult to pull that off in first person.

4. Another weakness involves showing the inner workings of characters other than the hero. The narrator can't delve into the minds of others or show what others think or feel.

5. The biggest weakness I see is that readers see all characters and events through the eyes of the protagonist, which means that even though the person may be perceptive, the other characters are usually superficial.

> Before I use the first-person POV, I ask myself,
> "Is it the best way to tell my story?"

Four Viewpoints

*

SECOND-PERSON POV IS THE LEAST USED and the most difficult to write. "You open the door and immediately see the face you hate." That's second-person POV. Writers rarely use this POV in fiction because: 1) it's difficult to write well; 2) it sounds affected; and 3) it's not a natural way to tell a story.

Using second person is a type of first-person POV. It's as if the narrators talk to themselves. You can't inject your own comments or observations—the story belongs entirely to the second-person narrator. This POV is a nice gimmick for a short piece, but for an entire novel, it becomes wearing. Jay McInerney did it well in *Bright Lights, Big City*, but that's rare.

Here's the beginning of "The Beautiful Uncut Hair of Graves," a short story in David Morrell's collection, *Black Evening*, "Despite the rain, you've been to the cemetery yet again, ignoring the cold wind blowing against your pant legs and shoes."[14]

A few pages later, Morrell has his character driving along the Pacific Coast Highway and it reads: "Preoccupied, you barely notice the dramatic scenery: the windblown pine trees, the rugged cliffs, the whitecaps hitting the shore. You ask yourself why you didn't merely phone the authorities at Redwood Point…"[15]

Although the descriptive style is the same as it is in first person, you do have a little more freedom. Here's a made-up example to express what I mean:

You're wearing your size five dress that shows you at your best. Avalon Foundation hides the creases near your eyes when you smile. He stares at you and you know you've hooked him.

> I'll consider second person as slightly removed from first person.
> I won't use second person in fiction unless nothing else works.

---

[14] *Black Evening*, David Morrell (New York: Warner Books, 1999), p. 321.
[15] Ibid., p. 330.

Four Viewpoints
PART 9 OF 18

*

IT'S ALL RIGHT TO USE SECOND-PERSON POV in certain kinds of nonfiction. I recommend it when the article or book is instructional and I'm an instructor giving you information or explaining how to make something. You talk directly to the readers (as this sentence does to you).

Most of this book is written in second person. Perhaps it sounds boastful of me, but my reason is simple. I've been writing and selling professionally since 1971 and have published in almost every genre. Thus I feel I have the experience and credentials (my published work) to back up whatever I put in my book. (Notice I wrote "experience and credentials," which doesn't mean I know everything. I share with you what I've learned.)

You don't need years of experience to write in second person. But be aware that you're coming across as the authority—the one who knows—and you're writing to someone who is ignorant or knows less about the topic than you do.

Be careful that you don't come across as patronizing—and I know a few writers who do that unintentionally. You don't want to sound like the condescending authoritarian who says, "There is only one way for you to accomplish this. You must do it my way to be successful."

> When I write instructions or how-to material, second person may be a good choice.

Four Viewpoints

*

IF YOU WRITE IN THE SECOND PERSON, you address the readers directly, as in "You walk into the room and there she is, tall and blonde and looking like trouble." This is difficult to maintain for a full book and few writers can do it well.

You can intersperse first person and second person. I often do first person and mix it with second person. (I also switch from first-person singular and first-person plural.) In my book *Unleash the Writer Within* I frequently shift from first-person (singular or plural) to second person. I do it on purpose. In chapter 9, called "Weaknesses—or Gifts?" I start in first-person plural.

"Three of us went to a booksigning of an author I knew slightly."[16] I could have written, "I went with two friends" and it would be first-person singular. Or I could have written, "You and two friends go to a booksigning." In this vignette, I was the observer and wanted to tell people about Rick. I followed it with a story about a woman writer. I ended the section like this:

> In these examples I've presented two needy, negative-impact individuals. Their inner privation shows in what they write.
>
> But then, all of us express our neediness in what we write. I used those two examples because they seem obvious.

Unleash the Writer Within is a teaching book, and I wanted to turn from my POV to the readers (second person). I made a scene break and here's the next paragraph.[17]

> Think about your different strengths and weaknesses. Let's start with the premise that the two terms are opposite sides of the same issue. Your power is also your drawback.

---

[16] *Unleash the Writer Within,* Cecil Murphey (OakTara, 2011), op. cit., p. 38.
[17] Ibid., p. 39.

When I wrote in the first-person singular, my purpose was to tell them something about Cec Murphey and his experience. I shifted to first-person plural when I wanted to wrap my arms around writers and say, "This is how all or most of us feel."

When I want to instruct, I shift to "you" and it feels right to me.

Before I choose POV,
I'll make certain I define my purpose.

Four Viewpoints
PART 11 OF 18

*

AUTHORS USUALLY WRITE SECOND PERSON in the present tense. Ordinary observations seem stronger when you shift to second person.

Here's a comparison:

First person: I peer into my husband's musty study. The neatness tells me that no one has been there. I smile. *They haven't found the incriminating document.*

Second person: You peer into your murdered husband's musty study. The neatness tells you that no one has been there since his death. You smile. *They haven't found the document.*

The experts insist that the second sounds more ominous. By injecting murdered and death, they say it sounds more natural.

They may be correct, but it doesn't feel right to me. My point is that personal choice is the most significant reason for choosing a particular point of view.

I need to be comfortable
with whatever POV I choose.

Four Viewpoints

*

HERE ARE A FEW CONCLUDING THOUGHTS on using the second-person POV.

1. You is the same as I. Here are the same sentences from two different POVs.

"As you approach the house, you see that someone has broken the lock. You push the door open and the noxious odor floods your nostrils."

"I approach the house. Someone has broken the lock, so I push the door open and the noxious odor floods my nostrils."

2. You write the narrative just as if the POV character is first person. You have to keep the "you" character's experience limited to what "you" can know.

3. You can write physical descriptions easily and it comes with a confident tone: "You stare approvingly at your suntanned skin. You flex your muscles and pose as if you've just won the Mr. Universe title."

If I write from a second-person POV, it can be jarring, so I need a good reason to use that approach.

Four Viewpoints

*

WE SPEAK OF THIRD-PERSON POV IN TWO WAYS. The most popular writing is done in what we call the *limited* third person. The other kind is sometimes called omniscient, universal, or unlimited third-person POV.

Third person limited POV shows readers only what happens around that person—usually the protagonist or heroic figure. If you start that way, you stay that way. (As I mention elsewhere, you can switch to first-person if you start a new scene. That's not common, but it's acceptable.)

You are always inside the perspective and emotions of one person. For most modern writing, you don't jump into another person's head within the scene. Everything that happens comes from that singular POV. There are usually frequent uses of "he thought," or "he said" from the narrator's POV.

I want to stress that readers see, think, and feel only what the main character experiences. There are no shifts to another character's thoughts or emotions.

> I remind myself that limited third-person POV
> is easy to read and the most widely accepted POV.

Four Viewpoints

*

ONE VARIATION ON THE LIMITED THIRD PERSON is to close a scene and open the next one from a different third-person perspective. This is becoming a popular way for writers to express a wider range of emotions, character development, and scope.

For example, Rachel is our POV and this is the end of the scene.

> "I love you and I'll always love you," Rachel said. Tears filled her eyes and she looked away from Cary.

You insert a double return (as we called it in typewriter days) or you can use asterisks. This shows the break in a scene. We now pick up the story and we shift POV to Cary.

> His body tensed and he started to embrace her. If I forgive her this time, he thought, it will be the same story again. She fails me and makes me feel sorry for her. "Your words mean nothing to me this time," he said.

I like this variation in fiction. I can identify with more than one person. I can "become" both Cary and Rachel.

The third-person variation allows me to provide a wider scope to the plot and to develop character.

Four Viewpoints

*

IN THE THIRD-PERSON OMNISCIENT POV, you take a panoramic view of the characters and events. The story doesn't unfold through the eyes of a single person, but we become part of an invisible, all-knowing, all-seeing narrator. This is also called the God view: It means you know everything. This point of view works best in a story with a complicated plot and multiple characters.

In the omniscient POV, you "drop in" on any of the characters. You can write from the hero's perspective on page 39 and stay with it until page 43 when you move into the heroine's POV. On page 45, you shift to the villain's perspective. You may vary viewpoints as often as you choose.

In the nineteenth century, those whom we now call the classic authors often wrote from an omniscient viewpoint. They skipped from head to head within a scene. Often they stopped the action to comment on the people, and some would even pause to say, "And now, gentle reader" or "Pity him, dear reader, who thinks of such evil."

Years ago I read this someplace (and forgot to keep the reference, for which I apologize):

> Humpty Dumpty didn't realize it, but he would soon have a great fall, and all the king's horses and all the king's men would not be able to put him together again. (Humpty didn't realize what was happening, so we're not in his POV. We're godlike because we know what's going to happen even though the poor fellow didn't.)

Although I know omniscient POV is a long-established style, I choose not to use it for modern readers.

Four Viewpoints

*

RECENTLY A FEW AUTHORS HAVE TRIED and gotten away with the totally omniscient POV. For emerging writers, we suggest avoiding this POV because:

1. Switching POV within a scene jars careful readers. It shatters reality because neither you nor your readers are omniscient.

2. Such pauses in the narrative flow tend to *tell* readers what you need to *show* them.

3. The POV continually shifts. The writing tends to become more impersonal because readers don't identify with and focus primarily on one character.

4. Readers aren't always sure of your major character. Recently I read *A Grain of Wheat*, written in 1967, which is considered a modern African classic by Ngui wa Thionog'o. The back of the book reads, "Set in 1963, *A Grain of Wheat* tells the story of Kenya on the verge of…independence. The novel focuses on Mugo…"

Mugo? I liked the novel immensely, but another character, Gikonyo, seemed as much the focus of the book until I read the last 30 pages. I also liked Gikonyo much better than Mugo and, for me, that change would have made a more satisfactory conclusion. I could argue that the author would have been wiser to go with shifting third-person limited POVs, but it was his choice.

5. The omniscient is difficult to pull off and keep readers with you. When well written, readers can enjoy all perspectives, but it's risky.

> I avoid the omniscient POV unless there's a compelling reason and I'm positive I can do it well.

Four Viewpoints

*

NO RULE EXISTS THAT SAYS YOU MUST STAY IN A SINGLE POINT OF VIEW. You can mix them from scene to scene. You might alternate from the hero's POV in one scene and the heroine's in the next.

You might write a chapter using third person and shift to first in the next. Rosellen Brown wrote a novel about a young man who molested and murdered his sister (*Before and After*). She arranged the book in four sections, with different viewpoints of the same story. We lived inside each of the four surviving family members. The reviews on Amazon were mixed and mostly negative. (Part of the mixed reactions may have been because of the theme.)

In which genre are you writing?

Examine books by authors who write in the same field. Familiarize yourself with their POVs. Ask yourself, "Why did they use that POV?"

I remind myself that it's easier to sell books written in the usual POVs.

Four Viewpoints

*

HERE ARE MY CONCLUDING WORDS OF ADVICE ABOUT POV.

1. Use first person if you want the entire book to have a limited, personal, and individual perspective.

2. If you want high reader identification with your character, first person is a good choice. Or go with limited third person.

3. If you want to describe your character *from the outside,* where you tell us "she thought" or "he said," limited third person works well.

4. If you want to experiment and can justify it, choose second person as a modified first person.

5. If you want perspective so readers can glimpse the attitude and feelings of several characters and grasp the plot from different outlooks or perceptions, the omniscient or unlimited third person might work for you.

If you're unsure, write a page or two in each POV. As you examine them and compare what you want to accomplish ask yourself, "Which of these POVs is the most satisfying to me?"

> I have to decide the POV
> that works best *for me.*

Don't Filter

*

OF ALL THE PRINCIPLES I TEACH IN WRITING, the concept of filtering seems the most difficult to grasp. I have not seen this in any writing book, and it's too subtle for those who aren't serious about improving their skills.

Let's start with the principle. When you are in the point of view (POV) of one person, you need to stay there, whether you write fiction or nonfiction, for the entire scene. The tendency is to move outside the POV and become the observer of the action instead of the actor.

This shows when we use words such as *saw, heard, observed,* or *noticed.* Here's a simple example where the POV is first-person singular: I heard Allison sigh with contentment.

You have moved out of first person and have become the observer of the action. To remain in the POV, you would write: Allison sighed with contentment. You couldn't know she sighed unless you heard the sigh. If you tell readers you heard, you're no longer in the first person POV. You are outside of Allison and you're telling us what you observed.

Here's a sentence in third-person POV: Anna could feel the floor shake as the opera chorus assembled on stage. The writer jumped outside the female POV person and told us what Anna experienced. Better: The floor shook as the opera chorus assembled on stage. By describing what took place, readers are aware that Anna felt it.

> Because I want to become an excellent writer,
> I will avoid filtering.

Don't Filter

*

TO AVOID FILTERING, YOU NEED TO BE AWARE of staying within the selected POV. When you are in the POV of one person, readers see/hear/sense *only* what that POV person does.

When you tell us what s/he saw (or heard or any of the other senses), you pull us outside his/her POV. Don't tell us you felt. Show it from inside.

Here are five examples to illustrate filtering. Each becomes a stronger sentence if you omit *noticed, watched, feel, heard,* and *knew.*

1. Helen noticed he laid his strong hand on Eva's shoulder as he spoke. (He laid his strong hand on Eva's shoulder as he spoke. Helen is our POV person, so anything that happens in the scene comes through her senses.)

2. He watched her cautiously step back. (She cautiously stepped back.) He had to see her actions to know it.

3. I could feel my surfboard begin to slip. (My surfboard began to slip.)

4. She heard the door swing open. (The door swung open.)

5.Dorian realized precious seconds were ticking away. (Precious seconds ticked away.)

As a serious writer
I diligently avoid filtering.

Don't Filter

*

DON'T FILTER BY SHIFTING TO YOU. Some writers filter by switching to the second-person point of view. That's like a scene in a film where a man is ready to ring the doorbell to pick up his date. After he got to the door, before he could ring the bell:

Heather opened it and smiled. You know that warm, tender smile that makes a man know she was the one he wanted to marry.

Shifting to *you* is like that ploy actors use when they're in the middle of a scene and turn, face the camera, and talk to the audience. It spoils the scene. It pulls us out of the mood and the action.

- When you live in Los Angeles, you're not quite sure which scenes are for real and which could be performances.
- If you have ever been to an Itzhak Perlman concert, you know that getting on stage is no small achievement for him.

Are the sentences understandable? Yes, they are. But they're stronger if you stay in the POV that goes before it:

- Those of us who live in Los Angeles are not...
- It's no small achievement for Itzhak Perlman to...

Because I am a good writer,
I avoid shifting to *you*.

Don't Filter
PART 4 OF 4

*

QUESTION: WHAT ABOUT "HE THOUGHT" AS A FILTER?

Answer: It works the same way except that to write I thought or I remember is so commonly used in writing, it seems to have little effect.

You can avoid that construction by resorting to what we call interior dialog or monolog.

I could never love Tim, I thought. He's so reckless.

I could never love Tim. He's so reckless. Traditionally, you wrote interior dialog in italics because there were no words to indicate they were thoughts. Some publishers now put quotation marks around those statements.

Try to avoid "I remember" and you can often do that.

Example: I remember the night we first met. We were both caught in the rain.

Change: The night we met, we were both caught in the rain. (Obviously you remember.)

The best writing is subtle.
Readers may not consciously know, but I do.

7
* * *

Blocked Writers

You Don't Have to Accept Writer's Block

*

MY DEFINITION OF WRITER'S BLOCK is the temporary or chronic inability to produce new work. It's common—but definitely not a passive condition. Most writers soon move past the resistance. For others, writer's block is extreme and they're unable to write for years. They may even abandon any attempts to write.

Some brilliant person said that writer's block is a loud scream from the unconscious that tells you something is wrong.

I often tell people that I once had writer's block and it was the most awful, terrible, horrible hour of my life. My point is that you don't have to suffer from writer's block. You can stop it.

Here's a question I ask myself:
What is going on inside me that prevents me from writing?

Don't Have to Accept Writer's Block
PART 2 OF 15

*

HERE ARE TWO IMPORTANT THINGS I want to say about this condition.

1. Writer's block isn't laziness. It's not procrastination. Think of it as writer's *resistance*, which makes it an opportunity to take action.

2. Writer's block sometimes means you're striving for impossible or unrealistic goals. Or you focus on your manuscripts and not being good. Those two things can prevent your moving forward.

> I don't have to accept writer's block as either a temporary or terminal illness.

Don't Have to Accept Writer's Block

*

I'VE SPOKEN WITH OTHERS ABOUT THEIR STRUGGLES with writer's block, especially after they've been able to move on.

Sometimes the best cure may be for you to relax and not write. You may be under stress and being under stress means feelings of anxiety and perhaps fear.

I write books—that's how I make my living. I've learned that I can hit the pedal and hold it on top speed for several months. I also know that I can't sustain that indefinitely—I don't want to try. In 2010, for example, I produced six books before the beginning of November.

I stopped working and scheduled almost no speaking engagements until February. That may seem like a long time, but I felt emotionally depleted and wanted to rethink what I was doing and where I wanted to go. That is, I avoided writer's block by pushing writing aside for a period so I could read, think, and look at life with renewed vision. It worked for me; it might work for you.

One way for me to stop writer's block is to see it as stress—and eliminate the stress.

Don't Have to Accept Writer's Block

*

I'M NOT A PERFECTIONIST, but I know many writers who are. They can't stop revising their manuscripts and they keep trying to make every sentence better. They'll never make it good enough to meet their demanding selves.

Fairly early in my career, I had the tendency to hold on and continue to rewrite even though I couldn't see anything to improve my manuscript. In a month or a year, I could probably do better, I reasoned, but not now.

That's when I made a commitment to myself. When I worked on a manuscript (in those days I was a member of an editing group) and couldn't find anything more to change, I sent it out.

In the early days before I released my writing I had to say to myself repeatedly, "This is the best I can do at this stage of my development."

Even if my manuscript isn't perfect, when it's the best I can do, it's ready to send.

Don't Have to Accept Writer's Block

*

ONE OF THE MOST SERIOUS CAUSES OF WRITER'S RESISTANCE is *fear.* It can come in a myriad of forms. I want to point out a few of those forms I've observed.

Perhaps the most obvious is the fear that your writing isn't any good. You may not say those words to anyone and may defend your manuscript, but deep, deep inside you sense your writing isn't good. The worse you feel your writing level is, the more difficult it is to create words on the screen.

"If I write something and people read it," a member of the Scribe Tribe once said, "everyone will realize how bad I am."

"Or they might discover how good you are," I said, "and you are."

To my knowledge, that man has never published. He surrendered to an irrational fear.

As a serious writer, I face my fears.
Even if I think my writing isn't good enough,
I continue to write.

Don't Have to Accept Writer's Block

*

LIKE THE REST OF US, YOU HAVE A CENSORIOUS VOICE in your head. It's a form of self-protection and warns you when you're ready to do something foolish or against your values. Sometimes that censoring nag is too finely tuned and prevents you from being open to others, but even worse, it keeps you closed to yourself.

That voice whispers, "If anyone else knows you think such thoughts, they'd shun you forever."

The voice I fight says, "This is simplistic and everybody knows that. You're insulting them." I've learned not to listen to that belittling voice, but many listen—and stall.

> The protective voice inside my head
> may be too protective.

Don't Have to Accept Writer's Block

*

"I DON'T HAVE ANYTHING TO SAY," a would-be writer told me at a conference. "I want to write, but there's nothing there." That certainly made her different from the hundreds of people who truly have nothing to say but want to tell the whole world.

After she admitted she came to the conference to learn to open up, I said, "Obviously you must have something urging you to write, or you wouldn't waste your time and money."

"That's true, and yet I feel paralyzed when I try to put it down," she said. "I'm forty-two years old, married with two children, I never went to college, was a stay-at-home mother, and I have no work-experience credentials. Who wants to read anything I have to say?"

We talked for several minutes and I don't know if I helped, but I told her that she had lived forty-two years. Life experiences count—in fact, in many cases, they count more than the diplomas people hang on their walls.

Writer's block in the form of fear tells me that I have nothing to say.

To become a good writer,
I stand up to false self-accusation.

Don't Have to Accept Writer's Block
PART 8 OF 15

*

WRITER'S RESISTANCE HITS SOME in the form of repression. If that sounds like you, it means you have things to say, but you just can't put them out for the public to read.

Here's my experience. Twenty years ago, I contracted to collaborate on a book with a man. He had marvelous insights and I enjoyed working with him.

A month before I turned in the book, he called and asked me to take his name off the book. The reason came down to this: "I believe this now, but later I may change my thinking. If it's already out there in print, I can't unwrite it."

I tried to reason with him and point out that all serious writers change. That is, they grow. If they grow, they may not believe exactly as they did before or may change their position on something.

I also pointed out that most people probably wouldn't remember anyway. It didn't matter: He was adamant and I removed his name.

As a growing writer, I can change my thinking.
I mature. I learn as I live.

Don't Have to Accept Writer's Block

*

I OFTEN SEE A RESISTANCE that shows itself in two significant ways. The first is fear of failing. "What if I can't pull off my ideas? What if I fail to say it right?"

By contrast, there are those who fear success. "Suppose I write a book—a really good book? Then I have to do it again. I don't know if I could do it again."

We've all known of people who have written one wildly successful book and never wrote again. *To Kill a Mockingbird* is one example.

My response is, "So what? What's wrong with having one great success? Isn't it better to have one big success than ten failures?" Even though I speak those words, they rarely impact. Such people have given in to a fear of being successful. Until they figure out how to get beyond their barricade of resistance, they probably won't write.

Fear of failure. Fear of success.
Neither will paralyze me.

Don't Have to Accept Writer's Block

*

I REMEMBER ONLY HIS LAST NAME AS MILLS, but he joined a writer's group called the Scriptiques that I ran for nearly four years. He was fairly talented and he might have become a well-known writer.

But he couldn't take criticism.

He read our comments on his manuscripts and listened when we spoke, but when he sent back his revised manuscripts, he hadn't changed anything.

Mills finally left our group. He had a number of excuses about how busy he was and that his wife didn't like his spending so much time on writing. But we knew they were only excuses because he couldn't face the reality that his writing was good—but it would never be really good without a lot of improvement.

I think he was incapable of moving beyond writer's resistance because he couldn't accept criticism. The more our group pointed out his weaknesses, the less he wrote.

A few years ago I formed an online writers group and one member named Candy was talented—and her gift was evident, even though her skills weren't that advanced.

Whenever I edited her material I pointed out her weaknesses (and there were many) but also reminded her that she could learn the rules of writing. Each time I mentioned how much I admired her talent.

After five months, Candy dropped out. "You never have anything good to say about my writing. All you do is criticize. I can't take any more of your negativity." I never heard from her or about her again.

It was sad that she didn't seem to grasp the many good things I pointed out. Her inability to accept criticism blinded her to all my positive words.

> I learn to accept criticism
> and don't give in to writer's block.

Don't Have to Accept Writer's Block

*

I MET DANNY AT A WRITERS CONFERENCE which he attended every year. He had an excellent nonfiction book, but he had never written the final chapter. Editors had read portions and wanted the book, and so did several agents. But Danny never finished.

He knew what he wanted in the final chapter and he told the editors and agents, but he couldn't write that final portion. At the time, I thought Danny was unique; he wasn't. I hear this regularly from people who get thumbs-up from editors or agents but never finish. Danny finally figured out why he couldn't finish—why he resisted. "I was depressed before I began to write. That depression went away while I worked on the book. I'm afraid that if I finish the book the depression will return."

I started to reason with him and stopped, because I sensed that nothing I said would help. He'd probably heard all the arguments and suggestions before. I reminded myself that Danny had to make up his mind if he would allow his fear of returning depression to keep him from finishing the book.

I have a talented friend who has started fifteen books (possibly more). He has never finished one. His reason isn't the same as Danny's but the result is.

Some writers are afraid to finish a writing project.
I won't allow fear to block my creativity.

Don't Have to Accept Writer's Block

*

WRITING AGAINST OUR VALUES is the way I say it. Some people have laughed, but I'm convinced that we do that. Sometimes good writers take on a project because the publisher wants them to do it.

I almost got caught up in that. I felt flattered when the senior editor of a publishing house came to me with a writing project. "I know you can do it and do an excellent job." I loved hearing those words and I agreed. But something didn't feel quite right.

For the next two days I struggled over that decision. I finally called the editor, told him how much I wanted to work with him, but I couldn't do the book. "It goes contrary to my values."

He wisely listened until I finished. "I understand," he said.

By contrast, one of my friends received a large advance for a book that he couldn't write. He finally broke the contract, and it destroyed his relationship with the publisher. He told me, "I was writing something I did not feel, did not believe, did not care about, and I avoided writing what I did care about."

> If I try to write against my own value system, my wise, inner critic tries to block me.

Don't Have to Accept Writer's Block
PART 13 OF 15

*

YOU CAN'T REALLY SOLVE THE PROBLEM OF RESISTANCE or blockage as long as you consider your internal resistance as bad or evil. Or you blame outside causes such as your work schedule, your family, even say the devil is hindering you.

This isn't to argue, but if that sounds like you, here's one question: What if you accepted the inability to write as a *positive* emotion? What if you viewed your resistance to write as a gift from your inner self?

Here's how I say it: "The inability to write is a sign that your unconscious self is fighting with your conscious self." Perhaps you become excited about a project or a topic and want to write about it. And it's a good topic.

It may not be for you, or it may not be for you *now*. So you founder and can't seem to push yourself. Like others, you may resort to a lot of caffeine or other stimulant. I suspect that's why some famous writers became alcoholics.

Instead of fighting yourself, what if you paused and listened to your inner voice? What if writer's resistance isn't punishment, or an outer force working against you, but instead a wise inner voice—maybe even God? What if the resistance is a call for self-examination and moving forward?

I accept writer's resistance
as a positive sign to examine myself.

Don't Have to Accept Writer's Block
PART 14 OF 15

*

YOU CAN FIND GREAT JOY IN WRITING. It may seem strange to write about joy in the midst of writer's resistance, but I think the secret of being a productive, serious, and committed writer is that it brings me immense joy.

It's fun.

I'm often emotionally drained at the end of the day, but I've enjoyed my day. I've created words that become sentences that grow into paragraphs. I write words that people read—and often like what I say.

You might think of it this way. The pleasure you find in writing is the positive sign that it's your gift, your calling, your destiny. Good writing doesn't come out of rigid self-discipline. (Notice, I said *rigid).* You need to invoke self-discipline to write, especially in the early days.

If you have to force yourself to write or grumble because you don't have enough time to write, or feel you're neglecting more important things, you might do well to turn off your computer.

I've been writing and publishing for nearly forty years. I began to write shortly after I finished seminary and had entered a doctoral program. I discovered so much pure joy and inner satisfaction through my writing that I lost interest in earning a PhD. I dropped out of the program and I've never regretted that decision.

Joy and pleasure in writing
are excellent antidotes to writer's resistance.

Don't Have to Accept Writer's Block

*

LET'S TALK ABOUT OVERCOMING THAT POWERFUL, INNER RESISTANCE. The first, most obvious thing about it is to call the affliction by name.

"I'm blocked."

I read various writers who tell us to leave our writing, go for a walk, or watch TV. I have no objections to those suggestions, but I think they miss the point of writer's block. What they suggest often works, but it only cures the immediate illness and doesn't get to the cause of the disease.

It's not a matter of needing to distract yourself. *You're blocked for a reason.* You can begin to trudge forward once you admit the resistance.

The next step is to ask a significant question: *What is going on inside me?*

This is no capricious or evil emotion. This inability to focus comes from inside and wants to help you and not hold you back. Don't try to analyze what's going on. Focus on *what* and ignore *why.*

It's not enough to ask the question, you also have to learn to listen for the answer. I can't tell anyone how to listen, but I know that for those of us who aren't used to looking inward, it's difficult.

It's not impossible.

I ask and keep on asking until I learn the answer.

Some people speak of it as praying—and that's exactly what it is. I avoid using the word with this topic because prayer for many is perfunctory and ritualistic. If asking and listening for a response for you is prayer, make it a cry that comes from the depth of your being.

> I overcome writer's resistance
> by asking myself the right questions
> and waiting for the correct answer.

8

* * *

Being Edited
and Editing Groups

Being Edited

*

AFTER I HAD BEEN WRITING FOR THREE YEARS and published more than fifty articles, the late Charlie Shedd met with the Scribe Tribe. Our editing group of eight writers met every third Tuesday evening and edited each others' material.

Charlie read the initial chapter of my first attempt at a book and spent twenty minutes dissecting my manuscript. It hurt to have him slash sentences I had written and rewritten ten times. But he caught things I hadn't seen.

Intellectually, I knew he critiqued my material; emotionally, I felt he criticized me. Although I've now published more than 135 books, I still don't like it when an editor rips apart my prose. No matter how hard I try, editors find ways to tweak sentences or delete words.

Here's something to remember: Unless you self-publish, someone will always edit behind you. Being edited is part of the being-published process.

If I can't accept editorial changes,
I don't want to write for publication.

Being Edited

PART 2 OF 6

*

EVEN THOUGH EDITORS IMPROVE YOUR MANUSCRIPTS, they want you to start with well-written articles and books. Everything you can do to make your own work outstanding not only sells the material, but it makes editors' work easier.

Too many beginning writers seem to think that if they write their material, edit it twice, it's ready to publish.

That's a good start, but not enough.

Trained editors can always find some way to help you improve your work. If you look good, they look good. But make it the best writing possible before you submit it.

My wife goes over my material. My best days are when she hands back an article without a red mark on it. That doesn't always happen, but it's becoming more common because I've worked conscientiously at this for nearly three decades.

For the first ten years of writing (or longer) hire or barter for a qualified professional to edit your manuscript before you submit it to a publisher. It will save you many rejections.

> I'll get editorial help *before* I submit a manuscript.
> I'll also accept help from the editor
> *after* I submit my manuscript.

Being Edited

*

To be successful as a writer, you need to realize that you'll always have things to learn. You'll never reach the place where someone can't improve your manuscripts. The struggle you may face (and many do) is that your writing isn't as good as you thought it was.

Writers sometimes beg me to read their manuscript and often say, "Just be honest. Correct anything you see."

They use the right words but rarely mean them. They usually mean, "Tell me how wonderfully I write." Until someone points out their weaknesses, they don't see them.

That's been true for me and I've become a better writer for having been edited. Although that's true, I wrote for several years before I could look at an edited manuscript and detach myself emotionally. It's likely true with you—and some writers never learn to be objective about being edited.

These days, my wife reads everything of mine before it goes out. Sometimes my assistant, Twila Belk, peeks at my manuscripts, and my daughter, Wanda Rosenberry, who is a copyeditor, reads them. Through the years I've learned to be thankful for Shirley's excellent eye. I'm embarrassed when a bad sentence sneaks past me; I'm grateful when she asks, "Can you clarify that point?" Twila or Wanda will ask, "Did you leave out a few words?"

Serious writers can find help and *they'll accept help because they're serious*. They can take online courses or correspondence courses; they can attend conferences; they can read books on writing.

You have such an abundance of resources available that it leaves you with no excuse for not improving. Consider joining or starting an editing group. It can be an invaluable learning experience.

Serious writers continue to learn.
Because I'm serious, I find ways to improve.

Being Edited

*

I DISTINGUISH EDITING GROUPS FROM CRITIQUE GROUPS. Members of editing groups *edit* each other's manuscripts. If they do it well, they learn more about the craft and become more sensitive to good writing.

In editing groups, members mark on the manuscripts—either with a pen, or on the computer they use comment boxes in Word texts. They do that before any face-to-face meeting, and no one reads manuscripts aloud after they gather. Since the proliferation of the Internet, more groups are moving into editing each other online.

I detest critique groups, and I'm quite vocal about it. Writers spend half the meeting time reading the prose aloud and members make comments. I consider that a waste of time. We write for the eye not for the ear (with the possible exception of poetry). Some writers read their manuscripts aloud to listen to the cadence and pick up sentences that don't flow, but that's different.

Editors don't sit and read submissions aloud. As they read across the page, they recognize the quality of the writing.

> I help other writers when I edit them;
> other writers help me when they edit my prose.

Being Edited

*

NO MATTER HOW LONG YOU'VE WRITTEN or how good your prose, others can see things you miss. When I first began to write, I invited several other eager-to-publish writers to join me in forming the Scribe Tribe. We didn't know much, but we shared what we knew.

Every person who remained in the Scribe Tribe at least five years became a much-published writer. One of the "graduates" is Marion Bond West, *Guideposts'* most-published writer. Suzanne Stewart's first book sold more than 200,000 copies. Two alumni have been full-time editors for two decades.

I want to give a few reasons I strongly advocate that you and every writer become part of an editing group.

1. *Good editing groups offer a diversity of capabilities, backgrounds, interests, and knowledge.* I'm not naturally analytical, and I focused more on word choices and sentence flow. Other members taught me to recognize logical progression and development of ideas. I became a better writer.

2. *Being part of a group allows you to receive and to give.* You learn from the others, but you also teach them. You see areas of their writing where you can help them. It's as simple as the teacher who said, "I never understood English until I taught it in high school."

3. *Being part of an editing group offers new writers a sense of identity.* You belong; you're not alone. You don't have to hide your writing. You meet with others who understand and struggle with the same problems. They encourage you to open yourself on the page.

The major reason I believe in editing groups is simple: they work.

Being Edited

*

HERE ARE ADDITIONAL REASONS for joining (or starting) an editing group.

1. *Being part of a group enables you to dig deeper into yourself.* As you pull from within, you more readily accept yourself and others. It doesn't matter whether you write theological texts, murder mysteries, or personal-experience articles. The more you write, the more your group enables you to look inward and examine yourself.

2. *You offer support and affirmation and become a true mutual-help group.* About the second year of the Scribe Tribe, I realized that we not only helped each other, but we also cared about one another. As members shared their writing, regardless of the topic, they shared themselves. I learned to appreciate and to care about them. They reciprocated; they cared about me.

Through the years, I've watched writers discover healing from childhood trauma, rape, incest, divorce, addiction, and countless other problems by writing about them. Many who didn't specifically address their issues found acceptance among other writers and that gave them the courage to resolve their problems.

> Do I *truly* want to become a good writer?
> I start with a willingness to be edited.

How Editing Groups Work

*

HERE ARE ADDITIONAL REASONS for you to join or start an editing group.

1. It's a humbling experience. Someone can always help improve your writing.

2. An editing group is one way for you to learn professionalism. Remember the principle: A group edits *my work; it does not criticize me.*

3. An editing group offers a sense of identity. You're no longer alone in your desires and ambitions.

4. You associate with other people who can understand you and your dreams. An editing group can offer support and affirmation as you pursue your craft.

I join an editing group to learn from others and prepare myself to become an outstanding writer.

How Editing Groups Work

*

WHEN I STARTED THE SCRIBE TRIBE, I knew what I wanted to learn and I didn't want distractions or disruptions. The longer the group met, the more I was able to write guidelines to make us more efficient. I wrote the following advice for face-to-face groups, but most of this can apply to online groups as well.

1. Members commit themselves to: 1) submit a manuscript as often as the group agrees; and 2) edit each submission received.

2. All members submit manuscripts to each other. Members agree to read all submissions and write comments on the manuscript. Then they will send the edited manuscript to all members.

3. Except in unusual circumstances (and all members must agree), we ask non-submitting members to leave the group.

4. On MS Word, members submit publication-ready manuscripts, such as double-spaced, 12-point font, one-inch margins, headers on each page, and starting the first page 3–4 inches from the top.

5. Members write editorial comments on the manuscript. They ask questions, point out difficulties, or suggest a different outline or approach. They often write a summary comment at the end of the manuscript.

> If my editing group works well,
> I improve—and so do the others.

How Editing Groups Work

*

1. THE EVALUATION SERVES AS PART OF THE PROCESS of learning the craft. Members strive for honest opinions, tempered with kindness.

2. Members don't tell others *what* to write. They try to help each other write better and to make manuscripts marketable.

3. No one has to accept or implement anyone's comments. (Take the ones that help; forget the rest.)

4. Members make no negative value judgments ("This is bad"), but offer suggestions for improving the writing.

5. Members won't repeat comments made by others. If they have nothing new to add, they will say so.

6. Meetings center on assisting members to improve their craft. Members agree to stay on topic and not divert the group from its task.

7. When members make comments, they will offer at least one positive comment. Writers need to know what they are doing well and what isn't working.

8. When the group discusses a person's writing, that person may *not* talk or comment. This guideline forces them to listen to the comments. It also prevents their defending their writing.

9. *After* everyone in the group has given comments, the person edited may ask questions. They will confine their questions to issues that didn't arise during the group discussion or about any comments they want clarified. *It is not a time to refute another's comments.*

> I am as kind and truthful with others when I edit
> as I want them to be when they edit me.

How Editing Groups Work

*

ONE PERSON ACTS AS THE EVALUATOR ON A MANUSCRIPT. This person is responsible to guide the discussion. Normally, each person leads the discussion on only one manuscript and encourages everyone to participate in the oral evaluation.

1. Set a time limit. In the Scribe Tribe we set twenty minutes for this task. If handled efficiently, that's usually enough time.

2. The editing begins with general comments on the entire manuscript. This includes structure, outline, beginning, plot, and conclusion.

3. Members use this time to speak about things they did *not* write when editing the manuscript.

4. Once each member has had the opportunity to make overall comments, the next step is a page-by-page discussion, including syntax, word choice, clarity.

5. After the page-by-page discussion, the evaluator asks for any closing or overall comments that have arisen through the editing procedure.

When I help other writers and they help me,
all of us improve our craft.

The Most Important Part
of the Sentence

*

THE LAST WORDS ARE THE MOST IMPORTANT PART OF A SENTENCE. Although you'll find this listed in Stunk and White's *Elements of Style,* and it's not a grammatical rule, it's a good lesson to keep in mind.

Think of the end of a sentence (and just as true with the last sentence in a paragraph) as your final, most emphatic word. This is a principle I didn't grasp until about 15 years after I began to publish.

As the author, *you* decide which words you want to emphasize.

I wrote these words in a first draft of my book, *Unleash the Writer Within:* I am a passionate person; I can be a passionate writer if I choose.

When I read the sentence again, I decided that the strongest part of the sentence should be *I can be a passionate writer.* It's the being and not the choosing that I wanted to emphasize, so I revised it to read: I am a passionate person; if I choose, I can be a passionate writer.[18] I felt that I not only emphasized the important word, it also gave the sentence more rhythm.

Here are examples from two of my students who didn't understand that principle:

- Richard rattled the bushes with a stick he broke loose from a tree on the way in. (Better: With a stick he had broken loose from a tree…he rattled the bushes. *Bushes* is stronger than the preposition *in.)*
- He heaved a sigh of relief, although drenched in fearful sweat. (Reverse the clauses. The sigh of relief feels stronger to me than the fearful sweat.)

I put the emphatic part of the sentence at the end.
Those words make the most impact on readers.

---

[18] Murphey, op. cit.

Two Power Positions

*

AS I'VE ALREADY POINTED OUT, in a straight, declarative statement, the final word is what we want to emphasize to the readers.

Let's see how this works by referring to a piece of advice a professional writer gave me when I was still new in the publishing business. Or I could say this stronger: When I was still new in the publishing business, a professional writer gave me a piece of advice. Both are correct, but it depends on whether I want to emphasize *publishing business* or *advice*.

Here's the advice she gave me, which will make this clearer:

1. If you're going to be a writer, you must be willing to walk naked *down the street*.

2. If you're going to be a writer, you must be willing to walk down the street *naked*.

Obviously, the second is stronger. *Down the street* isn't important and carries no significant meaning, so we sneak such weak words into the middle of the sentence.

As a writer, you determine which words you want to emphasize. Consider this statement: *No Such Grammatical Rule* or *No Such Rule in Grammar*. Which is the better, stronger word: rule or grammar? The answer: Whichever *you* want to emphasize.

I know what I want to emphasize in a sentence.
I place the emphasis in the correct place.

9

* * *

Those Awful Rejections

About Rejections

*

EARLY IN MY WRITING CAREER, I sent a manuscript to a large-circulation magazine and within weeks I received a rejection. Inadvertently, I sent the manuscript back to the same magazine. Two weeks later, the same editor not only accepted my article but also asked if I wanted to write paid book reviews. (You don't think I refused, do you?)

I'm not encouraging writers to follow my example but only to point out that rejection is a subjective response. The cliché holds true: "What one editor hates another one loves."

Here's another truism: If you're going to submit material for publication, you'll receive rejections. That's a guarantee.

At a writers conference in North Carolina in 2001, the speaker asked those of us who had received more than 10 rejections to stand. More than half the conferees rose. "How many have received twenty? twenty-five? thirty?"

As the numbers increased, fewer people remained standing. At the end, I was one of only three left. All of us admitted to having received more than 100 rejections. None of us felt embarrassed. In fact, one of them said, "Rejections are our red badge of courage—we fought the battles and turndowns are our wounds."

Rejection is an unwanted-but-necessary part of professional writing.

> If I can't handle rejections,
> I don't submit for publication.

The Impersonal No

*

ONE OF THE MOST PAINFUL LESSONS TO LEARN is that when editors say no, it's not personal. Editors and agents turn down the *material* and that makes no personal judgment about the *writer*. Although I knew that intellectually, for several years I went into an emotional downswing each time I received a rejection.

Why wouldn't you have emotional meltdowns? You throw yourself into the writing arena and you have to learn to separate the professional response from personal rejection.

Here's something I used to say when I received turndowns: This reflects the work I submitted; it says nothing about me as a person.

Don't allow rejection to shake your faith in your work or in yourself. (Your work may deserve rejection but that's another topic.) If you believe in something you've written, keep sending it out—a dozen times if necessary—until it's accepted.

Occasionally manuscripts are accepted after twenty or more rejections. In 2002, for example, I wrote a book for women whose sons, husbands, or relatives had been sexually abused. Every publisher I tried turned me down, although I got close one time. An editor wrote, "This book deserves to be in print, but our company will never do it."

In the summer of 2008, at a book trade show, Steve Barclift of Kregel Books told me he'd wanted to publish something by me for several years. "I have one book," I told him, "but you won't take it."

"Try me," he said.

I told him the idea and he said, "I'd like to see it." Kregel issued a contract, and in 2010, they released *When a Man You Love Was Abused: A Woman's Guide to Helping Him Overcome Childhood Molestation.*

The point is that I believed in the book and kept trying.

A rejection reflects the work I submit;
a rejection doesn't reflect on me as an individual.

Why Those Rejections?

*

WHY DO EDITORS REJECT YOUR MANUSCRIPTS? Aside from personal taste, here are what I consider the two most common reasons.

1. It wasn't well written. Too many writers seem satisfied with their work. Today the word *entitlement* reflects that attitude. "I worked hard on that article and I think it's good. Therefore..."

2. The writing or the material isn't distinctive. Here's an example of what I mean by that statement. A few months ago, I received a book manuscript from a writer who wanted me to endorse it. He was thoroughly orthodox and totally boring. Everything he wrote was true, but most of the illustrations probably originated with Tolstoy or Dickens. Today's writers need a fresh approach to any topic.

By contrast, a decade ago I wanted to write an article about getting an agent. That's usually considered ho-hum material because articles like that appear annually in most writers magazines. How could I make my article different?

I shifted focus and called it, "Why Would an Agent Want Me for a Client?" The editor bought it and I've had the article reprinted several times.

Was my article better written than others? Probably not, but it was distinctive. I took a different approach and that made it stand out.

I might not have anything new to offer, but I can write from a new, creative perspective.

Writing from Within

*

SOME MANUSCRIPTS ARE PUBLISHED that don't deserve it and we can point to many reasons.

A few years ago, an aspiring writer asked me to read a few chapters of his book. I did and wrote back, "It's as good as thirty other books; but it's not better than thirty other books." By that I meant it was all right. It wasn't particularly insightful and he wrote nothing significant that hadn't been said countless times.

Whenever I hear agents and editors at conferences, they say they want excellent writing. By excellent, I think they mean more than cleverly crafted sentences. They want a *distinctive voice* as well. "Say it to me in a fresh way" is my interpretation.

I'll tell you *the* secret to distinctive writing: It comes from within and expresses the depth of your soul.[19] The best kind of writing occurs when you speak from your heart (it doesn't have to be autobiographical). It's called being authentic or transparent. Too many writers can't do that. They have an insatiable need to be accepted, liked, or admired and those needs become more important than being true to their convictions.

Be you.

> I write from who I am
> and what I believe.

---

[19] I cover this topic more thoroughly in my book *Unleash the Writer Within* (OakTara Publishers, 2011).

Still Facing Rejection

*

IF YOU ASSUME YOU'VE WRITTEN WELL, are transparent, and have an excellent piece, you still face rejection. The first book I wrote for Don Piper, *90 Minutes in Heaven,* has now sold more than five million copies in English and has been translated into nearly thirty languages. It stayed on the *New York Times'* best-seller list for four years.

Very nice. However, five or six publishers turned it down before editor Vicki Crumpton was insightful enough to see the potential.

My point: Rejections happen. Every publisher has turned down projects that someone else bought and the book became a best seller. If you're a serious writer, you'll be rejected. Every editor won't like your writing style or your approach. Your job is to discover one who appreciates what you have to offer.

Years ago I met a writer named Art, who had written a fast-paced dramatic story about the Israel-Palestinian struggles. Twelve publishers turned him down. Al quit writing, because he couldn't handle the rejections.

Here's one thing I can say after a rejection: "I did my best."
Here's another thing I can say:
"Next time I'll receive an acceptance."

Other Reasons for Rejection

*

I WANT TO POINT OUT OBVIOUS REASONS why editors and agents reject manuscripts. Below are four additional reasons for non-acceptances.

1. The manuscript goes to the wrong publisher. Smart writers don't make that mistake. They know who handles which type of material. That also applies to sending manuscripts to agents for representation.

Go to their websites and see whom they represent. Look at their guidelines and they'll state what they don't want. Trust them that they know what they want to represent and will reject what they don't handle.

2. It's the wrong topic. *Newsweek* doesn't want personal-experience-testimonial articles. Sending them one is an excellent way to increase your number of rejections. Why would you send an article on divorce to *Marriage Partnership?* Some agents handle only fiction; others only nonfiction. One publisher loves speculative fiction, and another wants romance. Because you are a wise writer, you'll learn those things before you contact an agent.

3. It's the wrong slant (or treatment). *Focus on the Family* might like an article on abortion—but not if you try to present a pro-abortion stance.

4. The manuscript doesn't look professional. When editors get manuscripts that are single-spaced, filled with spelling errors, or written in 10-point Algerian or *14-point italics*, they know they're dealing with an amateur.

The thinking is that if those individuals can't present a professional looking manuscript, how could they write good material?

Professionals don't say to editors or agents:
"I know you don't publish this kind of material, but..."
I am a professional, so I learn where to send my material.

When It's Bad

*

I WANT TO POINT OUT THE MOST SERIOUS REASON FOR REJECTION: The writing is bad. Sometimes it's worse than bad. Editor Len Goss once said to me, "Most of the manuscripts I read are barely above the stream of consciousness." He meant the writing is slightly more than a continuous random flow of thoughts.

Many beginning writers submit material long before the manuscript is ready. (I know I did the same thing.) It's the best they can do, and it looks all right to them, so they take a chance. They also glut the delivery system and interfere with editors and agents who prefer to devote their attention to reading polished, better-quality work.

I can't tell anyone when a manuscript is ready, but I can offer suggestions. Here's my first and most important one: Have your work professionally edited—at least until you get established. It will cost you money, but it's an investment in your dream.

Go to a professional editor and not to an English teacher—unless you only want your grammar checked. Writing for publication sometimes violates strict rules. (I'm a former English teacher.)

After the edited version comes back, compare it with your original. Ask yourself why the editor changed your prose. A good editor makes your writing better; a wise writer appreciates the help.

Here's another tip: Never stop learning. I have two friends who were successful in the 1980s romance market. Today neither can get anything published. Neither kept improving. They sold books, but they stopped growing.

Keep finding ways to improve. Read about writing. Take courses if you can; read blogs and books on writing. Analyze what you read. Ask yourself why one writer speaks to you and another one bores you.

One warning. You can find dozens of blogs and ezines on writing. In all candor, many of them are the work of not-very-good writers. Before you accept suggestions from a blog or ask a professional editor to tackle your material, look at the person's credentials.

A few months ago, a woman emailed me that she didn't like the way I wrote and she was willing to become my editor. I try to stay open to someone helping me; however, she misspelled one word, had one run-on sentence of 43 words, and boasted that she had published five articles in an ezine. (Yes, she was also the editor of that ezine.)

I didn't doubt her sincerity, but I wouldn't have trusted her editing.

> Because I want to be a true professional,
> I seek and accept *professional* help.

Some Poor Writers Sell

*

"BADLY WRITTEN MANUSCRIPTS DON'T SELL." I said that once at a writers conference. Someone pointed out a popular-but-dreadfully written book. In that case, I agreed, but the truth is, an editor liked the writing. That doesn't excuse anyone for sending in less than the best.

Most agents accept less than 1 percent of submissions. Editors tell me that they toss back at least ninety manuscripts for every one they buy.

Just sending your material to more publishers isn't the answer. Even if fifty-three editors see the same badly written piece, the answer will be the same. Instead, if you have sent out a piece at least a dozen times and everyone rejects it, *assume* that you need to rework the material before you send it again. Get some qualified professional to evaluate it.

Some people are published because they can sell. If they would put a fourth of the effort into writing that they do into selling, they could develop into excellent writers. They use their sales figures as proof that they're good writers.

Some poor writers sell many books. That doesn't make them good writers. It means they are inferior writers who know how to sell inferior books.

I want to sell
because I'm a good writer.

Beating the Odds

*

RATHER THAN MOANING ABOUT REJECTIONS, I offer a few suggestions to beat the odds.

1. Make sure your writing deserves publication. This is an on-the-job training field. You grow as you write and publish more. Join an editing group. Pay a professional critique service to read and assess your material. Some material just isn't publishable no matter how hard you choose to work at it.

2. Resist the temptation to ask editors for a critique. Most editors don't have time. If you interrupt their work, they're likely to remember you—and turn down anything you send. Don't call editors and demand to know why they rejected your manuscript. (Yes, a few writers do such things, and some drivers text while driving.)

3. Be patient. Persist. Those who succeed in the writing business are those who keep at it for years, despite rejections and setbacks. Keep writing—and keep trying to improve. Read books about writing. Attend writers conferences. I know stories of people who went four years or longer before getting an acceptance. But in the meantime, they learned.

4. If an editor rejects the material but says positive or encouraging things, send that editor something else. If he/she says the piece came close, consider rewriting it and sending in the rewrite.

Rejections are part of the business of writing,
but they're only part of the business.

10
***

Literary Agents and Contracts

Let's Talk about Literary Agents

*

IF YOU WANT TO SELL BOOKS TO A ROYALTY-PAYING PUBLISHER, you probably need a literary agent. But first, a few words about royalties.

A publisher contracts for your book, edits it, produces it, distributes it, and usually pays you a small percentage based on sales. That part is easy to grasp.

What isn't simple is the way publishers figure royalties. Some base the royalty on the *suggested retail* price, others on the *wholesale* price. Publishers grant large discounts to Walmart, Costco, and other nonbookstore outlets. It's not uncommon for them to offer those outlets at a 75 percent discount on the retail price. When that happens, the authors' royalty rates are lower. (And it's all in the contract.) Regardless, they pay royalties based on the *net* sales.

Another factor is that sometimes publishers grant escalator clauses. That is, once a book has sold a certain number of copies, such as 50,000 or 100,000 they offer a bonus. (When my agent negotiated the contract for *90 Minutes in Heaven,* she, Don Piper, and I believed the book could become a big seller, but the publisher didn't. So because of my agent's savvy business sense, we received escalator clauses when the book reached certain sales figures.)

The royalty rates vary on hardcover, softcover/trade, and mass paper. Some publishers, especially the large ones, pay royalties each quarter, some twice a year, and most of the smaller houses send out annual checks.

They also send statements of sales—they're not always easy to understand and agents can decipher and demand clarification. That's another good reason to have an agent represent you.

Serious writers who sell books need literary agents to negotiate royalties. I'm a serious writer.

Some writers don't have agents and often boast about it. That's fine, but most of them could get better royalties and other concessions through an agent.

When I first signed with an agent around 1990, my agent insisted on things I didn't have the courage to ask for or the knowledge to consider. I'll give you a few of them.

The most obvious is the royalty rate. Sometimes agents can negotiate that, but not always. They can, however, find other ways to benefit writers. For example, free copies of books. Most publishers grant 10 to 75 freebies, but an agent might ask for 300. (That's the number of free copies my agent asked for and received for my second book with Dr. Ben Carson, *Think Big.*) Not a lot of money, but I sold or gave away those books for promotion.

Think of the importance of subsidiary rights. For example, I sold *Gifted Hands* before I had an agent. The original publisher was Review & Herald. They published the book in hardback and sold the subsidiary rights to Zondervan. The book has remained in print since 1990 in hardback, softcover, and mass paper. HarperCollins picked up the mass paper edition and sold 90,000 copies.

The downside is that Ben Carson and I receive only 50 percent of the royalties from Zondervan and HarperCollins. Standard contracts give the original publisher 50 percent of the royalties paid by the subsidiary publisher. Despite that, Ben and I have done well, but we would have done better if we had known.

Some publishers won't negotiate on the subsidiary rule and most of our books don't get picked up by another publisher. Even so, a good agent can sometimes get that 50 percent knocked down so the writer receives 70 percent.

Another area involves movie and electronic rights, as well as any other medium. When we sold *Gifted Hands,* Ben Carson insisted on retaining the movie rights. The publisher resisted but gave in and nineteen years later, Johnson & Johnson sponsored a made-for-TV version with Cuba Gooding Jr.

Good literary agents know the parts of a contract worth negotiating.
I pay them a commission so they bring in more money for me.

Why Is an Agent Necessary?

*

MOST AUTHORS DON'T KNOW EVERYTHING ABOUT PUBLISHERS, and need a specialist to assist them. A good agent brings access through her relationships in the industry.

Long ago publishers realized the value of agents, and most of them won't look at unsolicited manuscripts. They insist that all proposals come through a legitimate agent. You can do it, but it's not easy. You have to educate yourself and learn what you can expect. That includes understanding business terms and how sales and royalties work. Remind yourself that when you sign a book contract, you agree to a series of legal clauses that will govern your book for as long as it's in print.

You can become a successful writer without representation, but it's more difficult. It also means you must focus on writing your book, learning about the writing business, and pursuing publishers. You could have used that time and effort to start on a new book.

I'm a professional.
I seek professional representation.

How Do I Know When I'm Ready
for a Literary Agent?

*

I CAN'T GIVE A DEFINITIVE ANSWER, but I can make several suggestions.

First, of course, is to make sure you have a book and not just an article or two with a lot of fill-in material.

Second, get all the help you can before you're ready to submit. I can't emphasize strongly enough the value of a writers group that *edits* manuscripts. I know a few online groups and I expect them to increase.

Third, don't ask family members or friends to look at your book. They probably don't know about the writing profession. Don't ask published writers to look at your manuscript. They might be willing to do so, but if they do, please offer to pay them. They are professionals. You wouldn't ask your surgeon for a free gall bladder operation. Treat writers the same way.

Fourth, get professional advice. You can hire editors. You can go to a writers conference and get a 15-minute appointment with an editor or an agent. Some conferences offer "paid critiques." That is, a professional will read part of your manuscript or your proposal—for a charge—and give you written and oral feedback.

> I will actively pursue a literary agent,
> and I'll do so in a professional manner.

What Happens When Potential Clients Approach Agents?

*

THE BEST WAY I KNOW TO CONNECT WITH AN AGENT is at a writing conference. Check to see which agents are attending, research to find out who might be a fit for your particular project, then ask to set up a formal meeting.

If all the meeting slots are filled, try to approach them in line for a meal or between sessions. Most of them are happy to meet interesting people and always want to sign good clients.

No matter how you approach an agent, be pleasant, introduce yourself, and get to the point.

If you approach an agent at a conference, I suggest ideas to help make it successful.

- *Have* a *focus*. Although I'm not an agent, I do face-to-face appointments with writers. Frequently people sit in front of me and don't give me any direction on what they want to talk about. It's *your* meeting. Know what you want to say.

- *Prepare your presentation or question ahead of time*. Sometimes knowing how you want to start is all you need.

- *Be ready to talk about your writing*. Consider making statements to the agent that answer these questions:

   What's my idea?

   How do I show that's a strong concept?

   How is it unique?

   What's the market I want to reach?

   Why am I the person to write this?

If you can quickly hit the highlights, you'll find the meeting more productive and satisfying.

- *Bring a sample of your writing*. If the agent doesn't look at it, that's okay. At least you're prepared.

- *Listen*. If you're talking to a professional, listen to what advice that person has to say to you. Don't argue. Even worse is to say, "Yes, that's true, but…"

- *Decide what you want* so you can call the meeting successful. It's unrealistic to think an agent will sign you at a 15-minute meeting. Maybe you need direction for your story, to hear you're on the right track, or you want ideas on how to change your focus. Don't limit success to "signing with an agent or nothing."

- *Make sure your manuscript is ready.* One agent told me, "Most of the projects handed to me are somewhere between 30 and 70 percent ready."
- *Don't be aggressive.* Confidence in a writer is commendable; overconfidence turns off agents. They've heard it all before. Strike a balance between "I know I can do this" and "I'd love to learn from someone who is farther down the path than I am."

When I approach an agent or editor,
I'll know what I want to accomplish.

Attracting Agents

*

AGENTS THEMSELVES HAVE MADE THIS SUGGESTION: Learn about the agent before you make contact. For instance, Jeff Herman represents only nonfiction. Some agents won't take on children's authors. Make sure the agent you want handles your kind of books.

Find out how the agent wants you to make contact. A query letter? Email? Some want you to go to their websites and fill in the information. I don't know any agent who wants phone calls.

Work hard on your approach to an agent. Don't try to make it sound overly dramatic; make it sound like you. If you've done extensive research for your book, include that information.

Your query is a sales pitch but make it honest and realistic. "If you take the writing of *To Kill a Mockingbird* and combine it with *Catcher in the Rye*, you'll have an idea of the quality of my book." That's bragging and will probably repel agents.

I suggest you work on a summary statement, concept, or précis statement—what we sometimes call the elevator pitch. If you're in an elevator and have thirty seconds to tell an agent about your book, what would you say?

An agent sells for me,
but first, I have to sell the agent on me as a client.

Before You Sign with an Agent

*

Suppose an agent agrees to represent you. What then?

Some writers are so desperate for representation, they'll go with anyone. One writer said, "Once you sign with an agent, if it doesn't work, you can fire her."

True, but it's often painful. Besides, that doesn't sound like a professional approach. I suggest you hold off until you sense the agent is someone with whom you can work.

I have a number of questions for you to consider asking agents, or go to their websites and look for those answers.

- Are you a member of the Association of Authors' Representatives?
- How long have you been in business as an agent?
- If I want to contact you, how do you prefer I do that?
- If I make contact in your preferred method, how long should I expect to wait until I hear from you? If I don't hear within that period, what should I do?
- How do you keep your clients informed of your activities on their behalf? Will you inform me of all responses to my work? Do you do that as they come in or send me a list?
- Do you have specialists at your agency who handle movie and television rights? Foreign rights? Or are you proficient in those areas?
- Do you have subagents or corresponding agents in Hollywood and overseas?

Even though those are good questions, agents may not respond to them. If you go to their websites, you'll probably find the answer to many of them.

If you ask too many questions, you also risk the possibility that the agent may label you as HMA (High Maintenance Author) and choose not to represent you. Select the ones you feel are important.

> Before I sign with an agent, I'll learn about the agent. I want a long-term relationship so I want to be careful.

How Do I Sign with an Agent?

*

THAT SEEMS TO BE *THE* QUESTION FOR ASPIRING BOOK WRITERS, and it's a good one. However, having an agent is no guarantee of sales. It does mean a professional in the publishing business believes in you and your book. That's a great morale booster.

I've heard agents say they place 65 to 75 percent of their books. *Beware of those who claim higher numbers.*

Agents receive 15 percent of your royalty. Unless it's negotiated differently, publishers send the royalty check and statements to your agent. Your agent is responsible to ensure the accuracy of the accounting figures.

My agent has challenged those figures several times and won. It wasn't an issue of publisher dishonesty, but lack of understanding or ignorance. Every contract is different and sometimes the details get lost.

So how do you sign with an agent? First, find out who they are through writers loops; attend writers conferences; check websites. *Writer's Digest* puts out their *Writers Market Guide* each year. Most libraries carry the *Literary Marketplace* (known as *LMP)* in their reference section.

A number of specialty markets offer their own guide books, usually annually, such as *Children's Writer and Illustrator's Market; Novel and Story Writers Market; Poet's Market;* and *Christian Writers Market Guide.*

You can find many sites about literary agents. A few of them list those who've had serious complaints about them. Don't sign just because an agent asks you. For example, a scam agent, whom I know personally, was prosecuted by the federal government years ago. I don't know the outcome, but I recently saw one of his ads in a writers magazine, asking for writers to represent.

Ask your friends who have agents. Find out if they're satisfied. Ask if their agents are open to new writers. *Please* don't ask them to write a letter for you to their agent. If they want to do that, let them offer.

The AAR—Association of Authors' Representatives—is a voluntary organization of agents who subscribe to a code of ethics. They have an excellent website: http://aaronline.org/.

Here's another tip: When I read books by authors I like, in their acknowledgments, they often credit their literary agent. That's another solid lead. It implies that the agent likes that type of book and might be open to authors in the same genre.

Before you start your search for an agent, make sure that your manuscript is the best you can make it. It's worth the money to pay an editor or a proofreader or both. The manuscript may look fine to you, but to a professional, it may not.

> Before I seek a literary agent,
> I want to be certain that I'm ready for one.

Two Agent Questions

*

"FOR HOW LONG A TIME DO YOU SIGN WITH AN AGENT?" Cheryl asked in an email.

That depends on the contract the agent offers. And good agents *always* offer *contracts*.

If you have limited publishing experience but an agent takes a chance on you, the agreement can state that the agent will represent you for a period of one year or as long as two. The agent may have doubts about whether she can sell your book. If he hasn't sold it within the time limit, you're free to try another agent.

If the agent sells the book within that period and wants to represent you, he will usually become your representative until one of you severs the relationship. ("I write fiction and nonfiction," Marty wrote. "Should I seek two agents?")

A few writers have more than one agent, but it's rare. Most agents want exclusive representation, but it's more significant than that.

I've already written about agents and career planning. Becoming a well-known writer, a best-selling one, or a famous writer isn't easy and it takes committed dedication.

Think of it this way: After you've published your first book, you begin to attract an audience for your type of writing and in your chosen genre. Each time you publish, in theory anyway, you widen your audience. One agent said, "I expect it to take four books until my authors sell big."

Most readers, however, don't follow authors just because they're authors. *They follow them within a specific genre.* Fiction readers rarely turn to nonfiction and vice versa. (Writers are strange creatures so you may be an exception to most readers.)

It's extremely difficult to build name recognition in any field, but to try to sell both fiction and nonfiction makes it even more difficult. That implies writers work double shifts of writing *and promoting*. It rarely works.

Focus on one genre, stay with it until you have earned recognition. Then switch if you choose. For example, most of my 135-plus books are nonfiction. Over the past few years, I've published a few novels. Even though I had name

recognition among nonfiction readers, I'm having to attract fiction readers—
almost like starting from the beginning.

> Agents like an author who works in one genre
> and builds an audience.
> I want to be a writer whom agents like.

Agents and Your Career

*

I'M A STRONG ADVOCATE FOR LITERARY AGENTS—and they've become so much a part of publishing that I may not need to say this: Many writers don't realize agents do more than sell books.

Good agents care about your career. They rarely seek a one-book author. They want to sign writers who will produce many books that they can sell and continue to sell.

I've been with my current agent since 1997, and from the beginning of our relationship, we talked about my career. "Where do you want to go?" was one of the first questions she asked. We still talk at least once a year about my career.

Good agents know the publishing world and are aware of trends or needs long before writers. It's not unusual for editors to contact agents with whom they've worked and say, "We're looking for a book about…"

Agents act as buffers. That is, they have the expertise in negotiating, and authors stay out of the situation until they're ready to sign the contract. If authors have problems with the editors, the agents become their advocates. And differences do occur. It's comforting to me to know that when I have a problem with an editor I can appeal to my agent.

Editors move frequently. I read that the editors stay at one publishing house an average of 2.6 years. One editor may love your work but moves and her replacement may not and will make unreasonable demands—but you have an agent to stand up for you.

If I sign with an agent, that agent works for me
and makes my professional life easier.

254

Agents Handle the Money

*

EVEN WHEN AN EDITOR CONTACTS ME WITH A BOOK PROJECT—and that has happened many times—I don't discuss money. That's the job of my agent. Once an editor brought up the topic. "We'd like to work with you," he said, "but we can't give you the big, upfront royalties you're used to getting."

He didn't explain how he knew how much upfront royalties I received, but I said, "I don't care much about money, but my agent does. Talk to her." (He did and they worked out a contract that pleased each of us.)

When you sign with an agent, they take care of your finances, and they charge you nothing but the sales commission of 15 percent. Twenty years ago, agents charged for copying and postage because all manuscripts were on hard copy and went through the mail. Long-distance calls cost anywhere from five to ten cents a minute. In those days, many legitimate agents charged for the extras.

There's no reason for such charges today. If an agent wants to add charges for anything beyond the standard commission, don't sign.

I seek reputable agents who work on commission and only on commission.

Scam Agents

*

SCAM AGENTS ABOUND and they have a variety of ways of taking money from you and giving you nothing in return.

Here are some of the things to avoid:

Don't pay a reading fee. Agents read manuscripts—many, many manuscripts. If they're interested in looking at yours with a view toward representing you, they take the risk of reading bad manuscripts—and they receive a large number of them. They can also stop reading in the middle of page 1. I've heard that most agents accept less than 2 percent of the manuscripts they read.

Scam agents earn their money by charging reading fees; legitimate agents make their income exclusively from sales.

Don't pay retainer fees. I don't hear much of that these days, but it was an old method of asking clients to pay a small amount such as thirty dollars a month and it usually went on for a couple of years until the naïve writer figured it out and stopped paying.

Avoid literary agents who place ads in magazines or on the Internet. Good agents don't have to advertise. Most literary agents have more would-be clients clamoring for their services than they can handle.

Agents who advertise seem to accept anyone who offers a manuscript and charge a fee to read, but I've never heard of those agents ever selling anything.

Good agents have websites.

Don't give any serious consideration to signing with an agent who doesn't have a website. One questionable agency signs clients and then charges them $195 for the cost of setting up the writer's personal website. Even if the client already has a site, the agency convinces the writer that it's ineffective and he or she needs to pay for a good one.

Good agents gladly tell you the names of their clients, the books they've sold, and the names of the publishers. On their Internet site, one agency lists clients by profession and gives you first names only. My advice: Skip that agency, because there's no way you can verify their statements.

Good agents never, never, never refer you to a specific editing service. It's illegal for them to do that. They may suggest you get editorial help and come back, but they can't tell you which editor to contact.

If you have any questions about a particular literary agency, Google the name on the Internet. These days it's difficult for dishonest agents to hide from serious writers, but they still pull in money from the ignorant and naïve. Don't be either.

> If a literary agency tells me how easy it is to get published
> by signing with them,
> I don't want to sign with them.

Firing Your Literary Agent

*

PERHAPS IT'S PREMATURE FOR MANY WRITERS to think of parting with an agent. But it's good information to learn. Agents and clients do part company.

In 1996, my literary agent fired me. The relationship, although not hostile, hadn't been pleasant for me (and probably not for him either). Had I followed my instincts, I would have terminated our agreement two years earlier. I held back because, like many writers, I felt obligated—he had sold more than a dozen books for me. I worried that I might not find another agent. In the back of my mind, I foolishly wondered if he'd blackball me with other agents.

If we face the dilemma of *should-I-or-shouldn't-I-end-this?* we need to push aside our emotions and act on business principles. I saw that clearly when my friend Marilyn complained for more than an hour about her agent. When I interrupted long enough to suggest she end the contract, shock passed across her face. "He gave me my big chance. I wouldn't be a writer today if he hadn't sold my books."

"That's not true," I said. Even though I understood her feelings—I had been there myself—I wanted to do for her what I wished someone had done for me. "Did he receive his commission for the manuscripts he sold?"

After she said that he had, I pointed out that her agent didn't make her a writer. "He worked *for you* and sold a product over which you labored."

I can give advice like that because I've grown more confident and I know more about the publishing industry. When a relationship isn't right, the quality of the work suffers. Why deplete your creative energies by coping with bad business relationships?

A number of professional writers have since told me, "Having no agent is worse than having a bad agent or being stuck with one you don't like." They may be correct, although I disagree. Writers who have reached the level of professionalism are capable of getting a second agent. And if they can't, perhaps they need to market on their own.

Many (maybe most) career writers switch agents at least once.

> I may need to fire my agent,
> but I want to be sure before I take action.

Firing Your Literary Agent

*

BEFORE YOU DECIDE TO FIRE YOUR AGENT, carefully ponder the reasons you're unhappy. The common complaint is, "She isn't selling anything."

It may help if you remind yourself that agents don't make your books marketable. You may write remarkably well and be a steady seller, but that's no guarantee that everything will sell. Agents don't always sell everything they represent, no matter how persistent and assertive they may be.

My present agent has a manuscript of mine she couldn't sell, and the response we received is that the niche is too small. The fact that your work remains unsold doesn't mean that the agent isn't doing a good job. That agent may actually be doing an excellent job of representing you.

Here are a few questions to ask yourself as you consider switching agents.

1. Am I receiving copies of publishers' rejection emails or letters? Whether an editor rejects by email or a phone call, it's reasonable to expect copies or reports of these rejections. Some notify each time; most prefer to wait and send them monthly or at some other time.

You won't like reading what the editors say about your manuscripts—but at least you can document that your agent is circulating your work. Granted that many writers have fragile egos, but an agent owes you that information, even if it's only to say, "HarperCollins passed on your novel."

2. Does my agent pay royalties on time? Within ten days after a publishing house sends a check, writers should receive the statements and a check or notice of deposit from their agents. (My agent does a direct deposit within one business day.)

3. Is my agent difficult to reach? Is she lax about returning email messages or voice messages? If you speak with your agent and explain your dissatisfaction, that conversation may resolve the issues.

You probably won't be able to do it in person (the best way), so telephones are the next-best approach. Emails, faxes, and registered letters seem quite impersonal, but if you have no good communication, you may have to resort to the impersonal.

> Before I fire my agent,
> the first question to ask myself is, "Why?"

Firing Your Literary Agent
PART 3 OF 6

*

Misunderstandings occur, even in the best relationships. By speaking up, you can clear up differences. Unless your current agent is unusual, he has never taken a mind-reading course. That makes you responsible to communicate your concerns and unfulfilled expectations.

Your relationship may require only occasional adjustments. If you take the initiative, you might even have a fresh start in your joint business venture.

Be cautious about dropping your agent, but don't be foolish and hold on to an unhappy relationship. Over the years, I've talked with writers who have switched agents. In most cases, they probably did the right thing. In a few instances, the unhappy writer didn't like the second one any better. Or the third or even the ninth.

Here's my advice, which I wish I had followed myself before I signed with my first literary agent: Ask yourself, "What do I want from an agent?"

Or you might say it this way: "What kind of agent do I want?" Do I want someone who emails or phones every day? That's not reasonable, and most writers won't find such a person, unless the writer is getting mega-buck advances.

The agent who fired me didn't have a personality that worked well with mine: I'd call him bluntly aggressive. I wanted an agent whose personality reflected mine—someone I liked personally and assumed editors would as well.

Take time to ponder what kind of agent you want. During the period when I knew my relationship would end with my first agent, I seriously looked at the kind of personality I wanted to work with the next time. I needed someone whom I could email or phone and bounce ideas off and get a reply such as, "Sounds good," or "I don't think so," and then I could take the next step. When we signed, I asked specifically if I could throw out ideas by phone or email. She said yes.

I didn't need an agent who said, "Send me a proposal, and I'll let you know." I didn't want to invest a large amount of time into a product that wouldn't sell.

There are excellent reasons to fire your agent.
I want to choose the right one.

Firing Your Literary Agent

*

I WANTED AN AGENT I LIKED. Writing is tough and competitive, and I didn't want to deny the human element. Not only did I want to like my agent, I also wanted one whom editors liked. I know two highly successful agents who represent top clients, but editors have told me in confidence that they don't like them and dislike negotiating with them.

I'm fairly outgoing and straightforward. That's also the kind of person to whom I can relate. I wanted that magic something called chemistry. The first time I signed with an agent, like any inexperienced writer, I hardly knew what I was doing.

My story goes like this. One day an agent phoned me because a publisher had referred him to me when he wanted a ghostwriter. We talked for nearly an hour. A few days later, I received a contract from him.

The second time, because I had decided on the kind of person I wanted to represent me, I began to interview agents. I flew out of state and spent the day with one agent, set up tentative plans to drive to see another, and then I had lunch with Deidre Knight, who was then a new agent. Within ten minutes of our meeting, I knew we already had an intrinsic "something" that makes for a good relationship. I have been with her since 1997, and it's exactly the kind of relationship I wanted with an agent. And I've told her she will have to live another forty years so I won't have to seek new representation.

Estimates in the publishing world indicate that over a career span, writers average three agents.

When we remind ourselves that this is a business relationship, then it's no disgrace to the writers or the agency to make changes. Signing a contract with an agency isn't marriage. Writers hire agents to represent them. If a time comes when the employers feel they're not getting what they want for the money they pay, it's time to make changes. That is, it may be time to fire the agent.

"I like my agent and we're compatible."
Can you make that statement about your agent?

Firing Your Literary Agent

*

TIMING IS IMPORTANT. That is, don't wait until the relationship deteriorates so that you yell at each other or you detest getting an email from him. Or you wonder if it's worth sending a registered letter to learn if she's alive.

No matter when you sever the relationship, do it politely. Give as little offense as possible. Most agent-client contracts state that either person can break the relationship by letter or by a thirty- or sixty-day notice. Honor that contract. Be professional.

Even if you think the agent is cold-hearted, indifferent, and incompetent, treat her with respect and kindness. Offer the same courtesy you would like extended to you if the situation were reversed.

It's simple to break the contract. Make the parting as painless as possible. A phone call often is enough. If you can't do that, write a brief, businesslike letter to your agent and send it so that the agent must sign for it. (Obviously, you'll keep a copy of the letter and the receipt from the post office.) We like to believe that agents won't sue, but we now live in a litigious world, so who knows?

Begin by saying that you wish to dissolve the agent-client relationship. I suggest you provide no reason. To give a reason opens the case for argumentation. The agent may feel the need to defend himself. If you start citing reasons, you may end up writing rude or hurtful things. This is business, not a broken love relationship, and recriminations have no place in business.

It's never wrong for me to be kind,
even if the relationship between us isn't good.

263

Firing Your Literary Agent

*

IF YOU DECIDE TO FIRE YOUR AGENT, write a neutral, matter-of-fact letter to include statements such as:
- I wish you to stop making submissions of my work.
- For a period of sixty days, you may continue to represent me on any submissions that are still active.
- Please send me a list of all editors who have rejected my unsold work or are still considering any of my work.
- Please inform me of any offers or rejections that come as a result of those submissions.

If your agent has any unsold manuscripts, *which he has not yet submitted to publishing houses,* send instructions to delete, destroy, or return them.

After you end the business relationship, you need to realize that for already published work the agent will continue to receive royalties on your behalf and to forward statements. If they are representing work for you at the time you dissolve the relationship, it's still their project to sell—or they may opt not to do so. Ask them.

Nearly twenty years after the termination of my first agent contract, I still receive royalties on four books my first agent represented. That means he receives 15 percent of those royalties. That's how the book business operates.

Some writers don't seem to understand that the letter of termination only starts the process. *Until the agreed-upon thirty or sixty days have expired, you don't have the legal right to sign with a new agent or submit your work to an editor.*

A friend who had fired her agent that morning with a registered letter called me. The same day she queried an agent about representing her. It shocked her to hear that her letter to the prospective agent was both illegal and unethical. She was still under contract until the first one expired. Some agents write that fact into the contract.

When you fire an agent, you're taking a major career step. I urge you to get a lot of emotional support from your friends before you take that step.

If there are any mistakes and failures in my relationship, perhaps signing the contract was a more serious error than getting out of it.

What Are the Important Parts
of a Contract?

*

IN A GENERAL SENSE, THE TWO MOST IMPORTANT INGREDIENTS are clarity and completeness—that is, your book contract covers all the important issues, and does so in a way that you can understand.

Here are a handful of things I believe are important in publishing contracts.

1. A reasonable grant of rights. You own your words; however, you grant a license to a publisher to produce and sell them in some form, and the granting of rights details what forms that can take. Anything not specifically granted to the publisher is usually viewed as being retained by the author.

2. A clear expression of what you, the author, will do, which includes your due date, word count, and whether you're obligated to show them your next project or projects. The provision of art and photos, as well as your inability to write other books that may compete with your current book, and your willingness to sell other ideas to other publishers.

3. An explanation of the money they pay to you. You need to pay close attention here, whether or not you have an agent.

4. Details about the editing, production, and sale of your book. Make sure the copyright is in your name. It's reasonable to have the contract state that the book will be produced within 24 months or so after turning in the manuscript.

5. Make certain that you can buy copies of your own book at a reasonable discount.

> Although nothing in my contract is irrelevant, I'll especially watch the items important to me.

11

* * *

Making a Living as a Writer

Money for Books

PART 1 OF 4

*

YOU PROBABLY THINK OF RECEIVING ROYALTIES (MONEY) for books you write, and that is the usual method. The other method is called work for hire or sometimes a flat rate.

It's probably obvious, but the second term means the writer receives a specific amount of money for writing the book and a publisher makes that clear in the contract. For example, say you sign a work-for-hire contract for payment of $30,000 and the book sells a million copies. You still don't earn more. That's the risk. If the book sells only 8,000, you come out ahead with a flat rate.

Work-for-hire contracts are easier for publishers because they don't have to figure out royalty payments. Sometimes it's to a writer's advantage, but usually not. I did one deal where I received a flat fee and something like 3 percent royalty after the book had sold 100,000. The book was about 20,000 short of that goal, so I received no extra money. Here's something I learned early in my book-writing career: Whoever makes the contract has the advantage.

I remind myself that work-for-hire arrangements are usually written for the advantage of the publisher.

Money for Books

*

FOR ME, EDITORIAL RIGHTS are as important as the money issue. If you receive a flat fee, you have no input—unless you have it in writing. After you turn in your manuscripts, publishers can do anything they want with what you sent. They may not even list your name (and that happened to me a number of times).

Even if the publisher gives me a byline, I don't like my name on books where copyeditors can change things I've written without consulting me.

That's not to say that editors will attempt to destroy your project. They want to produce a quality book. However, they may not agree with things you write or may have your book say things you didn't intend. In that case, you have no voice or course of appeal.

The publisher may invite the writer into the editing process, but that's not a guarantee. Of the many work-for-hire arrangements I did early in my career, only twice was I invited to participate.

Am I willing to sell a book
without any voice in the editing process?

Money for Books

PART 3 OF 4

*

HOW DO PUBLISHERS DECIDE ON THE ROYALTY? That's a good question and here's the general rule: Publishers estimate the number of copies they project the book will sell the first year. They consider the author's experience, the genre, and the audience. They compare that book with the other books of that type they acquired in the past. They have a fairly good guess of how many copies they can expect to sell.

For example, you may have written a wonderful book to help people with cancer. Even if you receive a contract, unless you have a radically different approach, you're not likely to receive a big advance. Too many have written on the topic. That means, the publisher likes your book, wants to publish it, but doesn't expect to sell large numbers of copies.

Most publishers will also compare your book with what other publishers have done with similar books. They probably won't have the exact figures, but they'll have some idea of the success level of those competitive books (and those other books on the same topic are your competition).

Most publishing houses have what they call a pro-forma analysis program that calculates the cost of the editorial work. This also takes into consideration such questions as: What level of editing will your book need? You may have excellent content but you need a virtual rewrite or an editor (or someone else) will have to add more substantive material.

Another factor involves production cost. That includes the format, size, trim size, number of copies they'll do on the first print run. It will also include the royalty scale. Most publishers have their standard royalty rate until a book reaches a certain number of sales, such as 50,000 copies and then the royalty rate increases—and it will be so stated in the contract.

The amount of royalty the publisher offers me
is a good indicator of how well they expect the book to sell.

Money for Books
PART 4 OF 4

*

WHILE I WAS WORKING ON THIS BOOK, Rose Hilliard, senior editor at St. Martin's Press, asked me to point out the difference between royalty rate and advance royalty.

The royalty *rate* is based on sales of the book. The rate is generally the same with all publishers but there are exceptions.

The royalty *advance* is a percentage of what the publishers expect the author to earn in the first year, so they receive it in advance—that is, before they complete writing the book.

Most publishers pay half the royalty advance before authors finish the manuscript. They pay the second half when the publisher states, "The manuscript is deemed acceptable," as one contract reads. Another contract says, "Upon receipt of a satisfactorily edited manuscript."

This means that publishers edit the manuscript before they pay out the second half. That's important because some writers resist being edited. So it's a way of saying, "If you don't cooperate, you don't get the rest of the money." (It also implies that you have to repay the first part of the advance.)

A few publishers pay royalty in thirds and the final payment comes after they release the book.

Authors receive no additional checks until they have sold enough copies of the book to pay back the advance. The good news is that if the book doesn't sell enough copies to pay back the advance, writers don't return the advance.

A group of editors with whom I spoke at a conference, estimated that only about 20 percent of books paid back their advances. (Don't worry, the publisher won't lose money.)

> Advance royalty is what I call
> a good-faith payment by publishers.

How Do You Make a Living at Writing?

*

THE ANSWER: IT'S NOT EASY.

Think of the amount of time you need to put into writing a print book. Six months? A year? Probably longer. By the time you sell your first book and you ponder moving into being a full-time author, you're likely working on your next book. That's wise.

If you received a $100,000 advance for your first book (which isn't likely), you could live on that while you finish your second book. However, most first-time book authors receive fairly small advances, and sometimes none at all. They're unproven and no one knows how many books they can sell. Think less than $20,000—probably much less.

Could you live on that amount while you write your next book? Even if your first book sells well, you'll wait several months before a royalty check arrives.

My advice: Don't try to write full time until you're fairly certain you can earn a living. (If you have a working spouse or someone willing to support you indefinitely, ignore my advice.)

In 1984, when I made my career change to writing full time, I had earned an average of $14,000 a year for the three years before I went full time. That wasn't enough to support me, but I worked only part time, so I was sure I could make a living. I also had several books contracted before I made the change.

It's not easy to become a full-time writer. I'll consider this deliberately.

272

Is a Full-time Writing Career
for Me?

*

HOW MANY BOOK IDEAS DO YOU HAVE? To make a living in this business as an author, you must be a person who generates a lot of ideas and can put them into writing.

Most of the people I know who call themselves full time usually mean they have a supporting spouse or they have another occupation to pay the bills, such as teaching at a university or they're editors for a company. That's not bad or wrong, but it's not the same.

It's not easy to make a living in any of the arts. So why would you want to write full time? The pay is uncertain. You have no medical benefits, sick leave, and no built-in vacations.

I used to say, "I live by my wits."

Writing is a lonely, self-isolating occupation. I'm a people-person and not having others around was a difficult transition for me. I survived, but it wasn't easy. I have friends who do their work at Starbucks or McDonald's, but I wouldn't get any work done with such distractions around me.

Why do I want to write full time?
I need to answer that question honestly before I take action.

What Does Full-time Writing Mean?

*

WRITING FULL TIME IS MORE THAN JUST WRITING. It's also growing, researching, and marketing your books.

Is a full-time writing career for me? How many book ideas do you have? I'll state it again: To make a living in this business as an author, you must be a person who generates a lot of ideas and can put them into writing.

Why do I want to write full time? I need to answer that question honestly before I take action. Being a full-time writer is a demanding, full-time job and time consuming.

Think about what's required of you to make a living as a writer. You need to read a lot. I read at least a book a week and some weeks I sneak in five or six books—and I read eclectically and not just in my field. I read *USA Today* each morning and subscribe to a handful of magazines. I spend about ten minutes each morning learning (or relearning) something about the craft of writing.

I wrote the above to emphasize that you have to generate ideas—constantly. My agent referred to one former client, "He thinks every idea that floats through his head is a book idea. Most of them might make a 500-word article."

If I had not built my career on ghostwriting and collaborating, I probably wouldn't be a full-time writer. At the time of this writing, I have published more than 135 books, and slightly more than half are books I've written for other people. I wrote for them, continued to learn the craft, and earned my living.

For me, I had others giving me their material to write for them. That's not workable for most people. If I plan to make my living as a purveyor of words, I need to figure out how to develop new thoughts.

Am I committed to continue learning and seeking new ideas? If I'm going to write full time, I need a lot of ideas.

Making a Living as a Writer

*

I KNOW OF ONLY THREE WAYS to sustain a full-time writing career.

1. *Write at least one best-selling book*—a book that sells a million or more copies. That will bring in enormous royalties. Your next book, even if it flops, will be a decent seller because of what you wrote the first time.

2. *Write a lot of books.* If your books sell only 8,000 to 20,000 copies, you need to write many books to make a living.

To write a lot of books, you need to have a lot of ideas. Nora Roberts (who also writes under the name of J.D. Robb), probably writes more novels than anyone around today. She built her reputation with satisfied readers, who told more readers. Today, her name alone sells books. She continues to hit the top of the best-seller lists.

3. *Have many titles on the publisher's backlist.* This is an area most writers don't consider. Backlist refers to books previously published that you'll find in the back pages of publishers' catalogs.

Books on the backlist remain there as long as they continue to sell. I have at least a dozen on various publishers' backlist. One book that I published in 1990, with a small publishing house, still earns me about $100 a year. It's not much, but another book I published the same year still pays many of my bills.

I know three ways to earn a living as a writer;
I plan to use all three of them.

Marketing Myself
The Writer as Speaker

*

YEARS AGO, I DISCOVERED A FEW THINGS I DID WELL and determined to do more of them—specifically writing and speaking. Some people figure out what they do badly, stay at it, and (at their best) show mediocre results.

When it comes to the publishing profession, I'm smart enough to admit that I don't have the talent or the skills for marketing. Contrary to the advice I hear from others, I have no intention of throwing myself into months or years of mental drudgery for second-rate results.

However, I have a friend and a colleague, Kathy Carlton Willis, who owns KCW Communications **(http://www.kathycarltonwillis.com)**. She knows more about marketing than I'd figure out in years. I asked her to write this chapter to share lessons from her lifetime of learning as an expert in marketing.

Creating Speaker Promotion Materials
BY KATHY CARLTON WILLIS

*

One of the best ways to build your marketing platform is to get involved as a speaker for events. The most difficult part is getting the word out that you're available. You need to create promotional materials to make sure event planners have the information they need to decide if they want to book you.

Types of Promotional Materials
• *A speaker one-sheet* is usually a full-color glossy front-and-back flyer featuring the information you want disseminated. It's eye-catching and is easy to file away by event planners for future reference.
• *A tri-fold brochure* uses the 3 columns of each side as natural dividers for information you're sharing. It's visually appealing and can be easily mailed.
• *A rack-card* is the same size and paper as the cards you see for tourists at hotels. It fits in a business-sized envelope. It contains less content, but works well as an oversized bookmark. With the durable glossy cardstock, it lasts longer than most paper products.
    Pick the format that goes best with your branding, message, and purpose.

Information to Include in Your Promotional Materials
• Your name and contact information.
• Contract information for your booking agent (if you have one).
• Branding information, including tagline or main focus, and logo (optional).
• Your bio (written in third person).
• Endorsements (from attendees, event planners, and name-recognized experts or celebrities).
• Your key topic titles and blurbs.
• Current photo.

Other Items to Include for Event Planners
• *Demo recordings* (audio or video) in MP3, CD/DVD, or online.
• *Event kits*—a ready-to-use plan with the information they need to produce a

big event that includes tickets, programs, décor ideas, menu, music, and skits.

- *Publicity kit*—media information about the event.
- *Speaker contract.* Use a form to list your negotiated agreement, including honorarium amount, deposit fee, and travel specifications.
- *Handouts or other materials they can duplicate.* Provide print masters for the event planner to copy and distribute at the event.

The crucial factor in creating speaker promotional materials is to think like event planners. How can you make it easier for them to want to book you as a speaker?

If you have a PDF of your own speaker promo kit online, share the link.

Creating Speaker Promotion Materials
PART 2 OF 2
BY KATHY CARLTON WILLIS

*

Now that you have the design for your speaker-promotional materials, how do you distribute them? Here are suggestions to help you let the right people know about your programs and result in more bookings on your calendar.

Online Documents

Save your promo materials as PDFs and make them available online.

On your email to event planners, send a website link rather than an email attachment, which is often frowned on. It's also faster than sending print materials through the mail. Along with your own website, consider saving the PDF to a public document-sharing site such as googledocs or docstoc.com/.

Eblast Mailer

Redesign your printed promotional materials as an eblast. An eblast is a bulk email campaign that sends creatively designed materials in the body of an email. Eblast servers allow you to track who opens the email and who clicks on the links.

By phone, follow up those positive responders. They've already heard about you through the mailer, so your calls won't feel like cold calls.

Mailing Database

Compile a mailing database by researching contacts online and by trading lists with others who speak to similar audiences. Start local before you branch out (think Jerusalem, Judea, Samaria, and to the uttermost parts of the world).

A database is a spreadsheet with headers to reflect the contact information in a format that is mailer friendly. Use your database to send mailers with USPS or eblasts, and you'll have phone numbers for follow-up calls. Another option is to collaborate with a professional who has ready-made databases.

Hint

Pay attention to where others say they have been as guest speakers. For future reference, add those groups to your database. Fill in the blanks by using a search engine to pick up details you need, such as the name of group or church, mailing address, phone number, email address, fax, and contact name.

Don't wait for event planners to call you.

Become active, and you'll see an increase in the number of bookings on your calendar.

What Are Blog Tours?

BY KATHY CARLTON WILLIS

*

Blog tours work like commercials—like running the same ad on different stations to reach multiple audiences. They stimulate a desire for the book with the consumers you want to purchase the title.

Blog tours are virtual-book tours. Each blogger has a distinctive realm of influence—a different readership. The combined effect of being on multiple blogs in the same week helps increase your search-engine rankings and exposure. Some post the book information you send them; others write reviews in addition to the tour material.

How Do Blog Tours Fit into an Author's Overall Marketing Plan?

Blog tours develop a grassroots level exposure to the book, and create buzz because of the oldest PR method on the planet: word of mouth. Bloggers feature the book to readers the author couldn't reach any other way.

What Is Included in a Kathy Carlton Willis Communications (KCWC) Blog Tour?

We send bloggers an eblast that includes the information we want them to post on behalf of the author:

- Book summary and photo
- Author bio and photo
- Q & A style interview with the author, Top 10 List, or other extra features to personalize the tour and make the authors more approachable to the readers
- Details of any tour giveaways.

Creating Your Own Blog Tour

BY KATHY CARLTON WILLIS

*

1. Make a list of blogs and blog hosts to invite to participate in the blog tour.

2. Decide if there will be a giveaway. If so, in your blog tour invitation, list the details of the prize, along with a photo.

3. Create the blog tour content, and send it to the blog hosts along with the tour invitation.

4. To show your appreciation, mail a free book to each participating blog host.

5. Follow up with any blog tour hosts who need assistance in posting the blog tour so that it's customized for each host. Make sure they share the blog tour link (URL address) to their social networking sites, to increase traffic.

6. Mention each blog tour link on your social networking sites, and your blog.

7. Interact with the bloggers' readers on the day of the blog tour, and thank the host on the comments section of each blog.

Using Blogs as Part of Book Promotion
BY KATHY CARLTON WILLIS

*

Blog Ideas to Increase Exposure

At Kathy Carlton Willis Communications, we work with more than 600 bloggers, many doubling as book reviewers. You can use some of the same tips we use at our communications firm when it comes to deciding which bloggers to contact for book promotional purposes.

In Blogs, at KCWC, We Look for/Ask for

1. *A following.* Do they show a good number on their follower list?
2. *Good interaction.* Does the comments section show good reader/blogger interaction?
3. *Activity.* Are there new posts at least 4 times each month? We prefer 12 times per month.
4. *Social networking.* Do they plug the blog post links on Facebook, Twitter, LinkedIn, or to their mailing lists?
5. *Diversity.* Do they provide good content on their non-blog tour days, motivating their readers to visit frequently?
6. *Personalization.* Do they personalize blog tours to make them fit their readership? They might do that by writing a review or spotlighting an aspect of the book that makes it a good match for their blog niche.
7. *Book reviews.* Besides their blog activity, are they willing to post a review at one of the online bookstores such as Amazon?
8. *Quality content.* Do their views represent the same mindset you have? Look for well-written posts, well thought-out opinions, and wholesome conduct on their blogs.

We Help You Use Your Blog Connections for More than Blog Tours

1. *Reviews.* Bloggers write reviews in exchange for free books.
2. *Guest blogger article content.* Bloggers select from a variety of articles we provide for their sites. We provide reprint permission and make sure they also add a full bio, for promotional purposes.
3. *News releases.* When a news release is relevant to our bloggers and their

readers, we provide it in the form of article content. They can copy and paste the complete article to their sites, passing along our news.

4. *Contests and giveaways.* With new regulations, these require special legal wording, but can be done.

5. *Surveys.* We'll give bloggers a survey to participate in with their readers, using prize incentives to increase traffic. Blog readers vote on their favorites.

6. *Current content.* We provide article content that fits with an "awareness day" or water-cooler topic.

Are you using blog content to its maximum potential? Brainstorm new ways to add content to your own blog, and to the blogs of others that will reach your target audience.

Acknowledgments

Because I write about a lifetime of learning, it's impossible to remember everyone without listing thirty pages of names. But here are a few of the special individuals:

- Shirley has always encouraged me. She didn't doubt me when I left a secure income to jump into full-time writing.
- Deidre Knight has been my agent since 1996, and continues to have faith in me.
- The late Charlie Shedd saw my talent and told me I could become a writer.
- The Scribe Tribe stayed behind me during my first nine years of learning the craft. I especially smile when I think of Marion Bond West and Evelyn Campbell London and their invaluable feedback.
- Nick Harrison, an editor at Harvest House, has become a special friend.
- And special thanks to _____. (Please fill in your name because I want to make sure I acknowledge you.)

Real. Transparent. Honest. Gutsy. Straightforward.

UNLEASH
THE WRITER WITHIN

THE ESSENTIAL WRITERS' COMPANION

CECIL MURPHEY

Who You Are Determines What You Write.

You have unique stories to tell the world, teachings and words that will inspire and encourage others. So what are you waiting for? It's time to unleash that writer within.

This isn't your average writing book, with guilt-inducing lists of "how-tos" in your search to become a writer...or a better writer. Instead, internationally renowned and beloved writer Cecil Murphey walks as a companion alongside as you:

- Discover who you are.
- Develop your voice and writing style.
- Learn to write with heart.
- Become authentic to your readers.
- Grapple with the dreaded "Writer's Block" (it's not the deadly monster it seems).
- Harness the inner critic (and a few outer ones too).
- Expand your comfort zone.

The "must-have" resource for every writer
The perfect "retreat in a book" for writers events, discussions, and conferences

www.cecwritertowriter.com • www.cecilmurphey.com • www.oaktara.com

COMING SOON

The Promises of Ophelia Bennett
A NOVEL BY
CECIL MURPHEY

Trouble might not come right away, but it always came.
Of that truth, Ophelia Bennett had no doubt.

Northern Illinois, 1940

North Prairie School has a reputation for ill-behaved children, and veteran teacher Ophelia Bennett has just been offered a last-minute position to teach them. Desperate for a job to support her disabled husband, and with Superintendent Pettygill's intimidation tactics, she has little choice. If she refuses the demanding position, she'll never be allowed to teach in Illinois again. And, according to the manipulative superintendent, it would be her fault if North Prairie had to close.

Ophelia is confident she can change conditions in the school and love the needy children—she'd done it in her previous schools—but her unusual methods weren't well received by the community. She agonizes over what she knows will happen. How will she handle the jealousy and misunderstandings of the other teacher? What about the ambitious, difficult parents of the better students who would soon become her enemies? *Why do I have to do this again?*

On the first day of school, thirty-three students gather at North Prairie School to await the arrival of their new teacher, scheming how to make her miserable so she'll leave. As they size up Mrs. Bennett, they have yet to hear her promises that will change their lives.

Poignant. Heart-warming. Unforgettable.
A teacher's passionate calling to make learning easy and enjoyable.

www.cecilmurphey.com
www.cecwritertowriter.com
www.oaktara.com

About the Author

CECIL ("CEC") MURPHEY can't recall when he didn't want to write. Although he tried to get published first at age 16, he had nothing accepted until he was 38—"only after I'd learned a few things about the publishing industry," he says.

After Cec sold at least 20 articles, he made a double commitment to God and to himself: to never stop learning and improving as a writer, and to do whatever he could to help other writers. Thus began a lifetime commitment and passion to share with other writers what he's learned along the way. *Unleash the Writer Within* and *Writer to Writer* are his passions and legacies to all writers in the trenches.

Since his writing career launched, Cec has written or co-written more than 135 books, including the *New York Times'* bestseller *90 Minutes in Heaven* (with Don Piper) and *Gifted Hands: The Ben Carson Story* (with Dr. Ben Carson). His books have sold millions of copies, been translated into more than 40 languages, and brought hope and encouragement to countless people around the world. Cecil Murphey enjoys speaking for churches and for events nationwide. For more information, or to contact him, visit his website at **www.cecilmurphey.com.**

Cecil's blog for male survivors of sexual abuse:
www.menshatteringthesilence.blogspot.com.
Cecil's blog for writers:
www.cecwritertowriter.com.

www.oaktara.com